AT LEAST YOU'RE IN
Tuscany

A SOMEWHAT DISASTROUS QUEST
FOR THE SWEET LIFE

JENNIFER CRISWELL

GEMELLI PRESS

AT LEAST YOU'RE IN

A SOMEWHAT DISASTROUS QUEST
FOR THE SWEET LIFE

Published by Gemelli Press LLC
9600 Stone Avenue North
Seattle, Washington 98103

Cover design by Anahi Carrillo Felch
Typesetting by Enterline Design Services LLC

ISBN: 978-0-9821023-7-4
Library of Congress Control Number: 2012951387

GEMELLI PRESS

For my mom and my grandmother Nicolina,
two amazing women who inspired this journey.

A mia mamma e a mia nonna Nicolina,
le due grandi donne che hanno ispirato il mio viaggio.

ACKNOWLEDGEMENTS

This book is more than a tale about one year of my life; it involves a journey over many, many years, and so there are of course many, many people who have been instrumental in helping me along the way:

Mom, Dad, and my brother Matt, for being the original "Griswolds" and for always encouraging another adventure;

Cheryl and Bob, for being my New York family, for listening to me say "*ciao*" and "*pronto*" for years before I even moved to Italy, and for accompanying me on my Italian travels;

Susan Glasser, who told told me to stop dreaming of Italy and make it happen and who shared my passion for Italian men;

Janet, Bonnie, and Gill, my expat rocks, who know that a glass of wine and a piece of chocolate can solve many problems of the world;

Signe Pike, for reading every manuscript I have written and doling out miles of encouragement and advice;

Carol Billings, for yellow floppy hats, sharing stories on the terrace, and fine-tuning my right brain;

Daryl Warr, for believing in me;

Alessio Bordoni, Italian tutor extraordinaire, for having more patience than Job with my constant flubs;

Louise, for sharing my love of Italy;

Jessica and Jane, my book club/game night buds who good-naturedly read and gave me valuable input on my work;

Kenneth Hobbs, for loving Vin Santo as much as I do and for allowing me to use one of his beautiful paintings for publicity related to this book;

Marinella, for being the best neighbor anyone could ask for, a good friend, and *zia* to Cinder;

Antonella, Caterina, Giulia, and Rossella, for introducing me to the marvels of chatting on a stoop;

Angela, Laura, and Marisa, for being my first Italian friends;

Anna Fabroni and Federico Carletti, for Christmas dinners, holding my hand through the maze of Italian bureaucracy, and giving me my first real job in Italy;

and last but not least, Kari Hock and Michelle Fabio, *perché siete meravigliose e capite il mio senso dell'umorismo!*

PROLOGUE

Straightening my aching back, I gazed out over the rolling fields of lush green vines ripe with bursting dark purple grapes.

At least you're in Tuscany, at least you're in Tuscany, I repeated. My mantra.

But not even reminding myself I was toiling under the infamous Tuscan sun could save me from strongly considering fainting, stabbing myself, or at the very least, shamelessly feigning heat stroke now that I had reached day four of harvesting.

What would Lucy Ricardo do?

She was the only character I could think of who could've gotten herself into such a mess. Or maybe the blazing September sun was addling my brain. I'd signed up to work the *vendemmia*—the annual Sangiovese grape harvest in Tuscany—out of an innate sense of misadventure coupled with a desperate urgency to earn some money. Like Lucy, I'd managed to blunder my way into one of Italy's most venerable traditions in winemaking and was now floundering to find a way out. Sadly for me, my episode didn't include hiking up my skirt and stomping grapes. Nor was it only a half hour. Or particularly funny.

Instead, I was part of a *squadra* of twenty who were handed a pair of clippers and a bucket and told to start cutting.

For ten hours a day.

I bent back to my work now, a romantic sigh escaping me. The first day had been such an adventure. What does one wear to pick grapes, I'd wondered, as I plucked colorful T-shirts, a hoodie, and two pairs of jeans from my cluttered wardrobe, modeling them in front of my full-length mirror.

"*Faticosa*," friends had warned me over and over again. The work is tiring. Pshaw! I needed money. I'd ignored the small brown spiders that leaped into my bucket and only screamed once when swarmed by bees, angry that their fruit was absconding without their permission. I'd felt such sweet satisfaction as I'd filled bucket after bucket with fat purple grapes.

Then I woke up on day two, and everything hurt. My back was spasming, and my hands were so sore from gripping the clippers I could barely make a fist.

Aha! Now I knew why old Italian women were always portrayed as hunched over: They spent their days picking grapes. The only things keeping me from staying home were my pride and, of course, my circumstance. After five months in Italy without work and a spectacular breakdown in the middle of the main street, both money and pride were in short supply.

So I wondered, What would Lucy do?

A booted toe kicked the bucket next to me. "*Andiamo! Forza!*" Let's go! Come on!

I smiled gamely at Ernesto, the vendemmia leader, even as my body groaned, and hauled myself up to resume my place just as he told someone that rain in the forecast meant a pause in the vendemmia over the next few days.

"Excuse me, did you hear that?" I asked the woman on the other side of my vine. My Italian had improved, but this seemed too good to be true.

"Yes," she smiled at me through the foliage. "And we get paid today."

Hallelujah! Ignoring my blisters, I hacked at the overgrown vines with vigor. The grapes twined over their wire supports, creating a tangled mess; locating the point to snip required surgical precision. But by now I was pleased to find I could do this with some confidence. I was sticky with grape juice, a bee was caught in my hair, obviously confusing my tangled mess with its hive, and the growing heat of the day was determinedly focused on my sunburned shoulders, but I didn't care.

A few more hours and I'd be done . . . for this week. With a few more euros in my pocket, my Tuscan adventure would continue at least a little while longer—and I'd worry about next week, next week.

That's what Lucy would do, right?

CHAPTER ONE

IL SOGNO

It all began in Pienza ten years earlier. I was sitting at a table in the courtyard garden of my hotel, savoring a cappuccino and a freshly baked brioche. My last day in Italy. From beneath a flowering arbor of ancient grapevines flanked by vibrant pots of yellow roses, I inhaled the scents of the countryside: the heady smell of lavender hanging heavy in the morning heat, the aroma of olive tree trimmings burning in a nearby field.

Why did I have to leave? Bronzed and content after three weeks of traveling the country from Naples and Capri to Venice and now Tuscany, I scribbled down thoughts in my journal. An idea for a novel began taking shape in my subconscious. An Australian couple, newlyweds, sat at the adjacent table, debating whether or not to take a day trip to the nearby hill town of San Gimignano. I smiled thinking of Marco, whom I had met while hiking in the poppy fields outside San Gimignano's walls. An aspiring architect with eyes that never stopped flirting and the color of new spring grass, he'd taken me to lunch at his parents' *trattoria*. White, cottony fluff from the poplar trees floated around us as we laughed and devoured his mom's delicious *pasta al forno* while enjoying the scenery from a bricked courtyard. We spent the afternoon walking the narrow cobbled streets of his town, sharing a kiss in a tower high atop the city.

There's magic in that place, I thought. Go, I silently urged the newlyweds.

As the couple left the courtyard, a tiny brown swallow alighted on their table and began nibbling pieces of discarded brioche, unconcerned by the crunching of pebbles underfoot as the waiters hurried by. I grinned at him, enchanted.

Turning back to my journal, I let the weight of the words I'd just written settle, unsure what to do with them.

I don't want to be a lawyer!!!!! I want to write.

Over the past few weeks, this demand had floated up from an echoing place within me as I'd drifted in a rickety boat in the blue grotto of Capri, as I'd sipped an espresso in the eerie quiet of a Venice morning, as I'd licked melting gelato from my fingers while browsing the Campo de'Fiori in Rome. Being a lawyer hadn't brought me any such satisfaction. I wanted a life in which I didn't have to battle with attorneys who delighted in being antagonistic just for the hell of it. I wanted a life in which I didn't make people cry when I took their depositions.

The terror of admitting this to myself was surpassed only by the terror of wondering what people would say if I quit after three years of law school and only a few years of practicing law. Will they think I'm a failure?

But as I watched the morning sun glint off the stately cypress trees in the distance, I realized I didn't care. I wanted to do what I'd done since childhood. I wanted to write stories.

"I want to be here," I said aloud. The little brown swallow looked at me. And then he surprised me by flitting onto the chair beside mine as if to say, "Tell me more." I pinched off a piece of my brioche and slowly leaned across the table to put it within his reach. He eyed me speculatively for a second before hopping closer to take it. "*Brava*, Jenny," his head tilted in approval. "You're making the right choice."

This trip had opened my eyes to a different type of existence. I wanted to live in a place where even the birds took time to enjoy the small pleasures of everyday life. Where the men looked like demigods and even when dressed as Julius Caesar giving tours at the Coliseum had the confidence to invite me to dinner. Where the pace was slower, where meals were enjoyed. I wanted this life.

"Someday," I promised the swallow as I closed my journal and pushed back my chair.

"Someday, I'll be back."

✦   ✦   ✦

Lots of people dream of Tuscany. Most do the sensible thing: they rent villas with friends and spend their days touring the countryside and exploring the hill towns. They sip the wine, savor the food, and enjoy the same conversations of their regular lives . . . only in Tuscany. They ship home wine and olive oil and return with stories of their passionate tryst with a handsome Italian, or how they smuggled in fresh porcini mushrooms, content with their memories of a wonderful holiday.

There are fewer who actually decide to pull up roots and move to Tuscany. Often they are couples looking for a different life or who want to retire among the tangled peace of grapevines and ancient olive trees. They buy a centuries-old stone farmhouse to renovate and wax rhapsodic on the sweetness of the grass and idyllic pace of the countryside. We've all read those stories. The troubles with the locals, spending gobs of money so they can have all of their modern comforts. I loved them all when I read them too.

Then there's me. I moved here with an intrepid, aging Weimaraner named Cinder, perhaps with my own private dream but without much money. Without a plan. Without a safety net. And quickly discovered that not many people are idiotic enough to pick up and move to Tuscany under these circumstances.

It certainly wasn't the sensible thing to do.

My obsession with Italy began on that first trip ten years ago. Despite a couple of close shaves on a Vespa in Rome, being groped by an elderly tour guide on Capri, and a bike tour of Tuscany that just about killed me, I fell in love. I knew little of Italy's politics, and I had yet to watch my first Fellini film, but I felt an instant connection. Traveling around by train, bus, and foot, I communicated with a rudimentary Italian that was mostly food-based. I made friends, ate everything the gorgeous waiters insisted I try, and made a point of sampling every conceivable gelato flavor—including one with black pepper, which was surprisingly tasty.

It was this trip, during which I learned to say "yes" to every adventure, during which I'd felt romance and trusted my instincts, that convinced me that if I could muster up a little courage, I could chuck my legal briefs and follow my heart. To write. And to write in Italy.

My dream of Tuscany inspired me to start making changes. It took nine years, a move from Miami to New York—where I survived (just) as a dog walker on the Upper West Side—loads of Italian lessons, and three more trips before I hoisted sail on my Italian odyssey. But when you're meant to be somewhere, everything in between feels like you're treading water, just waiting for that wave to lift you and carry you onto the shore of your new land. My new land was Italy.

Marcel Proust said it of Venice, but for me it was Tuscany: "I made my dream my address."

Daydreams of my life in Italy floated somewhere between *Roman Holiday* and *My House in Umbria*: I would spend my days poking my hands into stone lions' heads, gobbling down gelato, writing delicious prose, indulging in a little too much wine of an evening, and being driven around the countryside by my confidant Quinty, who closely resembled a young Gregory Peck. I'd be cooking like a native, wholly embraced by my new and chosen town. Most of all, I dreamed that in Italy I would finally meet the love of my life.

Ha!

I hadn't foreseen wrestling with grapevines or hauling heavy buckets like a prisoner on a chain gang. I never imagined money-grubbing landlords or job offers with Dickensian-like conditions. I didn't think that tuna would become the mainstay of my diet because I couldn't afford much else. And I certainly hadn't considered that my personal life would become the talk of the town.

No, I was brimming with the optimism and energy that finds us at a new beginning when I packed up my life, my dog, and my laptop to embark on this journey. I saw myself through the eyes of my closest friends who kept telling me how brave and how adventurous I was.

Yes! Look at me! *La Regina dell'Avventura!* The Queen of Adventure!

OK, maybe it did take some *coraggio* to get here, but as I learned quickly enough, living a dream is very different from having a dream—and I was about to meet a whole different me along the way.

PART ONE

Paradiso

CHAPTER TWO

ARRIVIAMO

I peered through the intermittent arcs of the windshield wiper blades as we turned off the autostrada at the Chiusi exit, trying to locate the sign for Montepulciano in the drizzly gray cloak enveloping us. It was the end of April and a white fog shrouded the Tuscan hills, decreasing visibility to an alarming degree and making me thankful I wasn't driving.

As we wound our way up the mountain, the reality of what I'd done hit me like a blow to the gut, and for a moment I couldn't breathe. The pent-up emotion of the previous few weeks pricked my eyes, and I realized I was a few seconds away from sobbing in relief.

I'm here. I've moved to Italy.

My driver, Roberto, glanced worriedly in the rearview mirror. "*Tutto a posto?*" he asked.

I tried to smile reassuringly but said nothing. I didn't trust myself to speak. Roberto had a car rental company in Montepulciano, and my friends Laura and Gianni had recommended him to transport me and my trusty dog, Cinder, from the airport in Rome. Glancing over my shoulder, I caught sight of her, wedged between suitcases in the back of the minivan, and smiled reassuringly at her, too.

The fact that we made it this far was a minor miracle. Leading up to the move was a blur of working, sorting, packing, trips to the vet, preparing paperwork, and saying goodbye to friends, as well as all the hundreds of other things you do whenever you're moving; they'd left little time for contemplation. A Weimaraner of eleven years, Cinder hadn't handled the stress well. As our tiny

Manhattan apartment was dismantled piece by piece, furniture and belongings taken away by friends and Goodwill, poor Cinder morphed into a bit of a basket case, complete with a massive upset stomach. I spent the two weeks before our trip making pounds of rice and chicken, listening to ungodly gurgling noises in the middle of the night, spending exorbitant amounts at the vet that I couldn't afford, and worrying that I'd need to postpone our departure if I couldn't get her well.

"She's stressed because you're stressed," my veterinarian told me. But I knew better. Cinder was stressed because she knew no good could come of the gigantic travel crate set up in the living room. What all this meant was that each day leading up to departure was spent just putting one foot in front of the other and ticking things off my brightly-colored checklists, which were lodged under rolls of packing tape, scattered across the now bare parquet floors, and tucked between piles of clothing waiting to be sorted. Looking back, I'm surprised I could even find my oh-so-important lists.

By the time we departed, I couldn't remember the last time I'd had a full night's sleep. Nightmarish thoughts of Cinder traveling alone and afraid in the belly of the plane were enough to ensure a persistent wakefulness. Several friends had been disapproving of my taking an old dog on such a long flight; my best friend Cheryl was so upset she refused to come to the airport with us.

All things considered, it hadn't gone badly. The Alitalia staff and flight crew were attentive. At the check-in Cinder was treated like a minor celebrity with much fanfare and adoration. Cinder's sense of comic timing surely endeared her to the crowd; as I put my bags on the scale to be weighed, she attempted to climb up to be weighed too, charming the staff and inspiring much laughter among our fellow travelers in line behind us.

We descended into Rome early Sunday morning to an airport just waking and eerily quiet. The skies were spitting rain, and it felt unseasonably, almost unreasonably, cold. I raced through passport control to meet Cinder at baggage claim, trying to dispel my visions of her circling the baggage carousel, glaring her disapproval over and over again from the confines of her crate.

Luckily I spotted two airport workers wheeling in Cinder's crate as I reached the carousel. I sprinted toward her, whistling as I drew near, smiling at the look of relief on her face when she realized it was me.

We cut the plastic twist-ties I'd used to double and triple secure the door of Cinder's crate, and as she was set free and came bounding out, we had an emotional reunion straight out of a Hollywood film finale. The workers looked concerned, conferring in rapid Italian, as tears welled in my eyes. Cinder was panting heavily, her joy at being back on terra firma now mixed with an immense thirst and an urgent need to pee, both of which had to wait until I secured our bags. Cinder handled it all with good grace, making a mad dash for a sad clump of trees amidst the concrete of the airport short-term parking as soon as we got outside. She seemed fine and almost like herself as Roberto greeted us and loaded her into the back of his minivan. It was as if she knew that those few hours of misery were worth it because she was heading for retirement.

We spent the first half hour of the trip in silence. Despite four years of Italian lessons, my language skills weren't stellar, which made conversation with Roberto a tad difficult. My grasp on Italian was more of a slippery, sweaty-palmed, hanging-from-the-edge-of-a-building-with-no-sign-of-Superman-in-sight kind of thing. In other words, if I wanted to express my thoughts like a toddler, I was all set.

Mi piace. Non mi piace. I like. I don't like.

Voglio. Non voglio. I want. I don't want. You get the idea. If I wanted to say that I found the flight uncomfortable and turbulence was bad, I was out of luck. I could simply say I didn't like the plane. This would become a common frustration of mine as I settled into life in Italy, the inability to truly convey exactly what I meant because of a wanting vocabulary.

For some reason, on that first day it didn't occur to me that this lack of proficiency was going to be a problem. My Italian tutor, Alessandro, had assured me I'd be fluent within three months. I was skeptical since I'd spent most lessons flirting and drinking wine with Alessandro instead of actually speaking in Italian.

I attempted some basic conversation with Roberto, thanking him for coming down to Rome so early on a Sunday morning. He laughed and said at least there was no traffic. After another halting comment or two on my end, he quickly assumed responsibility for the conversation, telling me about his car rental business, then swiftly moving on to his love of hunting. Incidentally, learning the word "*caccia*" (hunting) would soon come in handy during my walks with Cinder.

As Roberto talked, he kept meeting my eyes in the rearview mirror as if trying to figure me out.

Ma quanto sei pazza? his light green eyes seemed to inquire. How crazy are you? He didn't seem to know what to make of this single woman picking up everything and moving from New York City to a small town in Tuscany.

Roberto had some of the physical attributes I'd grown used to seeing in the Tuscan men: handsome, wiry . . . short. Most reached about boob height on me. But what he didn't have was the local accent, which is as delectable to the ear as a delicious bite of lasagne is to the mouth. The sound is layered, evoking notes of heaviness, but it's also sensual and spicy, leaving the listener with an extreme sense of satisfaction. Any handsome Italian man with *l'accento toscano* drew me in like a moth to a flame.

"We're about ten minutes away," Roberto said. My stomach twisted in a mixture of anxiety and excitement, and I decided to send a text to my new landlady, Luciana, to let her know we'd be arriving soon.

When it came to Luciana, *non mi piace.* I tried to like her, honestly I did. She was a close friend of my Tuscan acquaintances Laura and Marisa.

I'd first met Laura when I stayed at her *agriturismo* (a working farm/bed and breakfast) four years before, having stumbled upon it by chance when looking for a place to stay near Montepulciano, my favorite hill town in Tuscany. We'd stayed in touch, and I'd been back three more times in the intervening years. Laura was fun, always chatting and laughing in an utterly infectious way, and worked nearly all the time. She spoke and drove faster than any person I'd ever met and was in the habit of crossing herself whenever she zoomed past the church of San Biagio, as though it could ensure safe arrival at her given destination.

Marisa was Laura's mom, who must have been in her mid-fifties but looked young enough to be Laura's older sister. In perpetual motion, she'd never be fat despite a sweet tooth that rivaled mine, and she had a decided flair for the dramatic. Every other utterance from her mouth was "*Che palle!*" or "*Porca miseria!*" *Che palle* literally means "What balls!" and *porca miseria* is "pig's misery!"; both are exclamations of frustration, disappointment, or downright anger and, although not profane, are not generally to be used in polite company.

My proficiency may not have improved much on that trip, but I could "*Che palle*" with the best of them. For example, imagine Marisa preparing a meal for thirty guests when someone calls to ask if they can bring two more people: "*Che palle!*"

But amazingly, cooking for thirty was not a huge deal for Marisa. The family used to own a restaurant, so her kitchen was modern and professionally equipped. Her stove bubbled daily with a *ragù*, her oven emitted a wonderful *profumo* of slow-roasting chicken or rabbit. Anyone who wandered into the kitchen was put to work spreading one of her special toppings on hundreds of pieces of bread for *crostini*. I spent my afternoons hunched over their sturdy herb-scented work table scribbling furiously in my tomato-stained notebook, trying in vain to capture the essence that is Marisa in the kitchen via her recipes. Back in New York, I finally gave up on the ragù, figuring I must have missed some essential ingredient, but I think I mastered her *zuppa di funghi*, for which I'd personally chopped hundreds of porcini mushrooms during the course of the week.

But all this brings me back to Luciana. Luciana had worked as Marisa's informal sous chef at the restaurant. On a trip I made before the move (to find an apartment, meet with the local *comune* (town hall) about my citizenship application, open a bank account, and locate a vet) Laura told me that Luciana had a small furnished apartment with a beautiful view she was willing to rent.

The air had been crisp and cold when we met Luciana at the apartment in the heart of the *centro storico* (historic center) of Montepulciano. Wood smoke wafted from nearby chimneys. We walked down a narrow street, herringbone-bricked and quaint, which ran alongside the town's main gate, La Porta al Prato. The houses were brick, some recently renovated, others a bit crumbly, but all joined together like a row of townhouses, each with its own intricate archway, dark green shutters, inviting brick balcony, and tile roof. Flower boxes graced nearly every window with a few hardy geraniums springing forth, even though it was the middle of winter. The immaculately clean street was void of people, but I caught the muffled noise of a television here or there as we walked along. It was a little after two in the afternoon, when everything in town shuts down and people tuck themselves at home to enjoy their *pranzo* (lunch).

Luciana was waiting outside the apartment, smoking. Tall and thin with almost masculine features, she was dressed in a blazer, blouse, trousers, and boots in various non-complementary shades of red, creating a look that was put together but at the same time decidedly unfashionable.

As she ushered us in, I drank in the tall ceilings with original wood beams, the sweetly appointed living room with chandelier, the gorgeous terracotta tiles. Luciana threw open the shutters, and a breathtaking view sprang into focus. I stared out the window, arrested, imagining sipping my morning coffee every day with that as my backdrop. Rolling Tuscan hills for as far as the eye could see, a patchwork of green and amber where cypress and olive trees met grapevines and farmers' fields. Another picturesque hill town loomed in the distance. Pienza, I wondered? The place where I'd begun dreaming of a life in Tuscany more than ten years before?

The landscape was surprisingly verdant even in February, such a stark contrast to the brown hibernation of the city parks I'd left behind in New York. And were those white puffs amidst the green actually sheep? I could already imagine the rosy blush of poppies that would be scattering the hillsides when I arrived for good in April. I felt a sudden urge to jump up and down and give a proprietary shout of "Mine!" (Family lore suggests I did this often as a child.) But nonchalantly, I pulled out my camera and took a quick picture from the window before trying to tune in to the conversation.

Luciana was explaining that the house had been her mother's, and after she died, they'd renovated it. My gaze wandered to an elderly gentleman seated in the corner. Luciana's brother, Luca.

"*Piacere,*" I said as he shakily rose, leaned on his cane, then kissed me on both cheeks, spouting in a garbled and rapid Italian. For some reason, I had a really hard time understanding older Italians, even their greetings, which were typically my strong suit. With Luca speaking so excitedly, all I caught was "*profumo,*" one of my kitchen words.

"He's saying you smell good," Laura leaned in with a smile. "And that the apartment is yours if you want it." Hmm. If all I needed to do in Montepulciano was shower to make an impression, I might do OK here.

As Luciana spoke, the smoke from her cigarette made her seem hazy and insubstantial despite her deep gravelly voice. Her head bobbed up and down between puffs as she and Laura exchanged pleasantries, her cap of brown hair three shades lighter than her black eyebrows. In the twenty minutes we'd been there, she'd smoked three cigarettes. I'm not a fan of cigarette smoke and briefly wondered how much of an issue that might be, living in a country of smokers.

But Fiddle-dee-dee, Jennifer, the Scarlett in me said.

No one was talking money yet, but I was invited to open cupboards and try the bed. I noted the washing machine and did a mental jig of happiness.

"*Completo,*" Luciana told me twenty times. "*Precisamente,*" she said, pointing out the freshly whitewashed walls. She wanted me to know how much care and time she'd put into the apartment to equip it with everything I'd need.

I nodded enthusiastically, mouthing to Laura, *It's perfect!,* and we agreed to meet again at the end of the week.

At the second meeting, I realized Luciana was a bit of a real estate barracuda. Laura had assured me that since Luciana was a friend of the family, the deposit would be minimal, and she'd even volunteered to help negotiate the rent. But it became clear after the first five minutes that there would be no negotiation. Luciana wanted three months *in anticipo,* plus the first month's rent.

Che palle!

In New York, two months' deposit was a more common request, and even that could be negotiated down at times. Luca was nowhere in sight for this visit, and I guessed Luciana had made him stay home lest he be overwhelmed by my *profumo* and try to give me the apartment for free. Laura frowned, her characteristic laugh nowhere in sight as she argued a point or two with Luciana. I wished Marisa had been able to join us. She would have been a more formidable opponent to Luciana's money-grubbing.

In the end, I wanted the apartment so I nodded and agreed to what Laura was telling me. I gave Luciana some cash to hold the apartment and confirmed she was OK with Cinder. I smiled and acted like I was thrilled she would be my landlord, but her aggression was shocking, causing me to sour on her. Plus, now I was in the hole—I'd brought along money for a deposit but I'd spent a chunk of it on a trustworthy cell phone when Laura told me not to worry about the apartment.

But now it was the end of April, and I was in Italy. Fresh start and all that. As we pulled up to the apartment, Luciana was waiting on the tiny terrace puffing away. It was still drizzly and cold but with Roberto's help we managed to unload the car in good time. Luciana stood by, cringing each time Cinder passed by, saying, "*Ho paura.*" She was afraid of my dog.

"It's OK," I assured her in Italian. "She's old . . ." and gentle? What was the word for gentle? But she didn't seem convinced. Roberto flashed me a look of commiseration as I paid him before he sped off.

Inside, the apartment was freezing. Couldn't she have at least turned the heat on? I pulled out the three months' deposit (less what I'd given her in February) and the May rent.

Luciana sat at the polished mahogany dining table in the center of the room, blowing smoke in my direction. She had one eye trained on the television where the Pope was giving morning Mass from Saint Peter's and the other on my hand, brimming with a colorful collection of euros. I slid into a seat beside her and handed over the cash, watching as she flicked ash onto what I assumed was one of my new dining plates.

She counted the money three times, brows furrowing. "*Dov'è il resto?*" The rest? Was she kidding?

"*Quello è tutto.*" I haltingly explained that these were the terms we'd agreed upon. My stomach churned. Was this some sort of scam and she wasn't going to let me have the apartment if I didn't pay her more money? I could already see the headlines: *Idiot American Gets Taken in First Hour in Tuscany.*

And then the last vestiges of my legal training kicked in, and I remembered something.

"*Ascolta*, Luciana," I said, plastering a smile on my face. Listen, lady. "You can't change the terms now. This is what we've agreed to. Plus, you've already told me you're planning to put a smaller amount in our contract than I'm actually paying you. Is that even legal?"

She puffed away for a few more seconds, brows knitted together, then crushed her cigarette and opened her arms wide. "There is no problem," she said.

"*Benissimo,*" I said. "So are we done here?"

She handed over all of the keys and then took me outside, pointing out the gas meter and a little cupboard under the terrace. "You can put the dog in there," she said.

I peeked into the dark, dank, tiny hole and somehow resisted blurting out, "*Stronza!*" I must be exhausted if I'm ready to call my landlady a bitch on the first day.

Luciana saw my expression and hastily beat a retreat.

I heaved a sigh of relief as I pressed the door shut.

"This is it, baby," I whispered to Cinder as I locked the door with a confirming double click, then cranked up the thermostat. "This is our new home." Cinder looked unconvinced, shaking uncontrollably and glancing warily around the apartment from her newly appropriated perch on the sofa. The day of travel had obviously left her out of sorts as well.

I sank down next to her, staring at the flickering light of the chandelier. Then two of the bulbs went dark. Cinder and I exchanged a look.

L'avventura had already begun.

CHAPTER THREE

BRAVE NEW WORLD

Some might call it foolhardy to pick up roots and transplant yourself to a new country without having all the particulars figured out. I'd certainly raised more than one eyebrow when I told friends what I was planning.

"But what will you do for work?"

"How will you get by when you can't speak the language?"

Or my favorite, "Aren't you afraid of getting fat from all that pasta?"

The more serious questions gave me pause or left me with some niggling doubt, but, being an optimist, I didn't like to linger too long in the parts of my vision that could only be seen in black and white.

Had I been concerned about moving to Italy? Of course. But my insecurities revolved more around what the Italians would think of me, my cooking skills, and my decidedly unfashionable apparel rather than any adjustment I'd be making to the way I was living day-to-day life. Each time I'd returned to Italy in the years following that first adventure, the connection I'd felt to the people and to the countryside was strengthened. *This is where I'm supposed to be.* I wasn't just picking up roots; I was planting them in the right spot.

I'm Italian on my mom's side of the family. Both of my great-grandfathers came from Sicily, and since I was a little girl I'd been conscious of the fact that I was Italian. I had the Italian grandmother who shouted "*Vaffanculo!*" at my brother and me with some regularity and who brewed coffee so strong my dad joked you could stand a spoon up in it. My grandmother was an excellent cook, and the smells of my childhood typically involved her "sauce" and onions and peppers frying in oil. The fig cookies she made every Christmas were an intensive labor of love, requiring the smushing of figs, various dried fruits, nuts, and honey through a meat grinder multiple times; sometimes it took all day and that was just the filling.

Her husband, my grandfather, died of cancer when I was four, so my only memories of him are of a gentle white-haired giant making me pancakes, and my mother taking me to the hospital to visit him before he died.

I inherited traits from each of my grandparents: from my grandfather, who was well over six feet, I got his height, his prematurely gray hair, and his shaggy eyebrows—mine were a bit out of control when I hit puberty. From my grandmother I inherited flabby Sicilian arms, a passion for cooking, an addiction to strong coffee, and a penchant for swearing in Italian.

After my grandfather died, my grandmother lived with us for half of each year, and in her room, which smelled sweetly of rose milk, hung a photo of four of my Italian ancestors—a typical stern, black-and-white affair from the early twentieth century. Dressed in somber clothing, they looked like they wished they were anywhere but posing for a family portrait, and all wore matching disapproving glares. I would stand transfixed whenever I was in her room. I was scared of them but still couldn't look away.

As it turns out, one of the people in the photo was my great-grandfather, Calogero Tulumello, who would eventually be the person responsible for helping me on my long, serpentine quest for dual Italian/American citizenship.

I reached into my battered leather backpack and pulled out the photo of Calogero and his wife, Emilia, that my mom had unearthed. I placed it on the wooden credenza in the living room. "I made it, guys," I told them. "I'm finally here."

I looked around my new home as I unzipped the first of my suitcases to begin unpacking. Had Calogero and Emilia's house in Sicily looked something like this?

This would be the first time I'd ever really explored an old Tuscan house. There were no closets to speak of, but there was a tiny sloped *dispensa* (pantry) off the kitchen where Luciana had shoved some brooms and a bucket. Cooler than the rest of the apartment, almost cave-like, the three-feet-thick walls of the cramped space made it a perfect place for storage. I already envisioned storing wine, olive oil, and all of the fruits and vegetables I'd be learning how to put up for next winter.

As I unpacked each item, I was almost giddy thinking, I'll just put this in my new wardrobe *in Italy*. Here is the shower curtain for my new bathroom *in Italy*. This is the first book I will read *in Italy*.

The apartment seemed bigger than I remembered, yet darker and different somehow . . . then I realized Luciana had removed some of the things that had made it "*completo*," including all of the throw rugs. Perhaps she feared Cinder would destroy them?

"The good news," I turned to Cinder, "is that she left us plenty of Virgin Marys on the wall. Who needs rugs, when you have *La Madonna* following your every move from each room?" Never one to get my sarcasm, Cinder eyed me pitifully. She was desperate for sleep but in her insecurity tried valiantly to keep one eye trained on me, like a cartoon character who'd soon resort to toothpicks to hold her eyelids open.

Unloading and unzipping bags, I realized that I'd brought mostly bedding. After trying the rock-hard bed in February, I'd been determined to stuff my feather bed and duvet into my suitcase. Unfortunately, having a comfy bed meant that I hadn't been able to bring much in the way of clothing. I had a few days' worth, but I'd have to get out to Laura's within the week and gather the boxes she'd been kind enough to allow me to ship to her. I sent her a text just to let her know I'd arrived, hoping maybe she and Marisa would stop by later.

Other than dried-up expired bouillon, some sugar cubes, and a bottle of *limoncello* that looked as if it might have been around since the end of World War II, there was nothing to eat in the house. Oh no. And it was Sunday! All the stores would be closed. I'd glimpsed a bar down the street, but how could

I subject Cinder to the trauma of being left alone in a strange place after her ordeal? She shivered from the corner, letting out a pitiful whine as if to confirm my suspicions.

By evening I'd crunched three stale Mentos from the bottom of my purse and ruminated over what desiccated bouillon might taste like. I can't believe I refused breakfast on the plane! At least Cinder had her food, which was starting to look pretty appealing.

I tried calling my closest friends. First Cheryl. No answer. Then Will. Ditto. What were they doing? Brunch at Henry's? Walking their dogs in Riverside Park? Over the previous few years, the three of us had been become virtually inseparable. Not only vacations, dinners, game nights, and margarita fests at our local bar, but the shorthand you develop with people you spend all your free time with, finishing each other's sentences, making the others laugh simply by repeating one word of a shared experience. They were my New York family.

Like Cheryl, Will hadn't taken the news of my leaving well, manufacturing lots of reasons not to spend time with me before I left. It was deeply painful, but on some level I understood. I was breaking up the gang. Lucy heading off without her Fred and Ethel. (Just to be clear, Will was Ethel—as the gay best friend, this was his right.) I knew Will had finally forgiven me when at my going away party he'd held up a gigantic map of Italy with the words, "We're giving her the boot!"

Next, I attempted to call my parents. Two calls and all I got was the unsympathetic digitalized voice of their answering machine. Were they the only remaining people who still used a real answering machine yet had never learned how to leave their own message? I grinned, remembering my dad's herculean efforts to hook up Skype before I left. A wave of homesickness for my family and my friends washed over me. I was so far away.

Was I really missing my old life after just a few hours in Italy?

Well, if I was, at least I was homesick in Tuscany.

I decided to distract myself with a bath. After five years of showers in New York, a nice long soak might be just the thing. I grabbed my towel and began hanging the Pottery Barn shower curtain I'd picked up after glimpsing the plastic, blue-bubbled atrocity that Luciana had provided. Oh goodness, I must have been so mesmerized by the horrid shower curtain that I didn't even notice that the bathtub wasn't full-sized. A sloped trough with a bump on one side for sitting, or maybe to balance yourself while shaving your legs, this tub left no possibility of "soaking" unless I wanted my knees to touch my forehead.

Sighing, I opted for a shower. Waiting for the water to heat, I headed to the bedroom to dig out something warm to layer on. Good God, it was freezing in here! I undressed hurriedly, reluctantly pulling off my toasty socks. My feet upon hitting the floor felt as though they'd just been dunked in a mountain stream. I shifted from one foot to the other as I gathered my clothes. "It's perfect in the summer," I echoed the words Luciana had repeated three times in Italian. "You won't even need air conditioning."

Sure, but what about winters? In my vision of life in Italy, I was plunked near a toasty fireplace, reading in the warmth, listening to the pleasant popping of fresh cut wood. If I'm really honest, I'll admit I was kind of hoping for an outdoor pizza oven as well.

Then I heard a loud *THUNK*, and I poked my head in the living room. That's funny. Cinder was sleeping and everything looked in order. I heard *THUNK* again, and the realization dawned too late.

I raced toward the bathroom. Oh my God! The shower head was possessed! Embodied by a maddened poltergeist, it slammed from side to side in the tub, water spraying everywhere. I reached to shut off the water only to slip on the freezing, and now soaking wet, slick tiles. Instinctively grabbing onto the curtain I'd just hung with an ungraceful lurch, I managed to pull half of it down with me, slithering to a heap on the icy floor. I was soaked, but thankfully I hadn't cracked my head open on the bidet.

Whew. I'd escaped death by toilet on my first night in Italy.

The only evidence of this little episode would, no doubt, be a humongous bruise on my backside, which I could already feel forming.

After a quick mop up of the sopping tiles, I finally took my shower. I peered out the tiny window and caught a glimpse of white puffs in the distance. My sheep were still there, nature's fluffy lawnmowers, methodically pruning the lush green hillsides. This immediately cheered me. But my relative tranquility was broken by a strange *whooshing* noise in the tub with me. That's not good.

I peered closely at the metal box suspended over one side of the bathtub, which Laura had explained was the water heater. There, through a tiny oval window made just for my viewing pleasure, I could see angry bluish-purple flames shooting up from inside. I have a little bit of a fire phobia (not the fire itself—see above wish for fireplace—but of being trapped in a fire) and somehow seeing flames dancing next to me while naked was not conducive to helping a phobia like this.

It took all of my effort—and a desire not to wipe out again—to stop myself from leaping from the tub. I remembered a scene from *Enchanted April* where Lottie's husband came to visit, and before his bath the staff of the house warned him not to touch the hot water heater as it is *pericolosa*, dangerous. He, of course, experienced this firsthand when the hot water heater exploded. So maybe this was normal? I didn't remember ever seeing this kind of contraption on previous visits to Italy, but it wouldn't be in the tub if it were unsafe, right? This was sure to be but one of many things I would have to get used to.

L'avventura, I told myself again.

I finished my shower with a speed that surely assisted the fight against global warming. As I gingerly made my way across the still-damp tiles with a level of caution reserved for icy New York streets in winter, I glimpsed one of the Virgin Marys on the wall of the living room. She seemed to be watching me with a wry amusement.

"OK, I take it back," I told her. "I obviously need all the help I can get."

✦　　✦　　✦

I awoke the next morning to the slow gong of church bells. First set, heavy and somber, and then another, more tinny and farther away. My house must be sandwiched between two churches, I thought. Once the bells stopped, I was surrounded by the happy tweets and twitters of birds, and as I scrambled to the window I caught sight of a flock of swallows, small, brown, almost bat-like when viewed in the predawn light. They dived and swarmed merrily, sometimes frenetically, as if in celebration of their return to Tuscany after a long winter in the south. My face stretched into a smile, and scooting back under the covers, I settled into my wrought iron bed and gazed up at heavy wood beams with large stucco bricks lodged between.

My unsettling disquiet of the previous evening was gone. My emotions had been right at the surface after the shower debacle, and I never did reach my family or friends. Laura hadn't called or stopped by. I'd felt small, far away, and alone. I'd literally crawled into bed and pulled the duvet over my head. Now it all seemed silly in the light of day. When I moved to New York I'd felt a little intimidated and off-balance in the beginning, too. This was surely the same thing, I naively thought.

Although the bells had just chimed seven o'clock, Cinder was still burrowed under her blanket snoozing. Maybe she was waiting to hear the sounds that usually greeted us in the morning: garbage trucks, sirens, screaming college students. Or maybe dogs experience jet lag too? Whatever the reason, in the ten years we'd been together, Cinder had never slept past six (and consequently, neither had I).

But as soon as she heard me stir, she poked her silky gray head out from under her blanket, realized she'd overslept, and began her elaborate routine of stretching and pacing. Obligingly, I threw on shoes and a coat so we could properly explore our new surroundings.

My front door opened onto a small terrace fifteen feet away from the nearest apartment, which had a brick-like façade like mine but looked recently renovated, whereas mine was being held together by the weeds that clung between the stones.

Peering through a small window, I admired the splashy orange walls. Something told me Luciana would never go for that.

We wound our way down a slender walkway, moss-covered and slick from all of the rain. The graveled parking area faced the countryside, a low stone wall protecting it from a steep drop-off. In the distance, Tuscan hills and valleys stretched out beneath us. Cinder pulled hard toward the wide stone stairs that angled down to the road below, and we set off on our first walk *in campagna* (in the country).

The air was still chilly, but the sun was attempting to poke through the clouds; a sweet smell like honeysuckle wafted from a broom-like vine of delicate yellow flowers. I inhaled deeply, like a dog with my head thrust out the car window—my body eager to expel ten years of city toxins. Bursting out of the wild grasses ahead were a clump of brilliantly red poppies, which for me symbolize Tuscany even more than the ubiquitous sunflowers. I stopped to appreciate the vivid papery petals.

Overwhelmed by where to begin sniffing, Cinder kept her nose to the ground, taking in everything: the grass, trees, flowers, holes, gates, hedges, other animals' scents, wild-eyed in delight. We walked farther from town, the houses alongside the road growing larger with pretty gardens lush with fruit trees and flowers. We passed a sign that read "*Divieto di Caccia.*" Thanks to Roberto the taxi driver, I knew that *caccia* was hunting, and as I glanced around the isolated countryside, I hoped the sign meant "No hunting" and not "Hunters welcome: Walk your large breed dog, which could be mistaken for a boar, at your own risk."

We continued to wind down the mountain, passing *un uliveto*, an orchard of olive trees, their silvery leaves not yet showing signs of the olives that would be ready to harvest in November. Tuscan olive oil. There is nothing like it. Forget any high-end olive oil from the grocery store. The taste of the bright green, recently harvested Tuscan olive oil, simultaneously fruity and spicy, is like liquid from the gods. If only I could find a job dipping hunks of bread into the local olive oil all day long. Talk about an ideal career match.

As Cinder paused, I glanced back up the hill, trying to locate our window in the distant buildings, and realized how far we'd descended. "We still have to go back up," I reminded her. "Let's pace ourselves."

The hill wasn't quite as beguiling on the way home; we walked on and on but didn't seem to be drawing any closer. My calves started to burn as Cinder and I panted our way up. They don't call them "hill towns" for nothing. I remembered passing a sign that said the grade was 15 percent, but I had no idea what that meant other than *steep*.

Back at the apartment I left Cinder to nap and headed out to buy groceries. But first things first . . . coffee. I beelined for the bar I'd seen the day before and bellied up for a cup of espresso.

"*Caffè*," I said confidently to the guy behind the counter, a cute Italian with floppy blonde hair and blue eyes behind funky glasses.

"*Caffè americano* or *espresso*?" Damn. Was my accent so horrible? Or maybe my orange Asics gave me away.

"Espresso," I said, now a little deflated. Then added, "*Non mi piace il caffè americano.*" So there.

He chuckled and turned to make my espresso. I looked around the bar, which was nearly empty. Modern and bright, it differed from some of the dimly lit bars of the historic area. Beside the counter sat a large display case of brioche and pastry delights, while behind it, shelves displayed bottles of every type of liquor or liqueur one could ever desire. A small dining area was neatly arranged with round, glass-topped tables flanked by glossy rattan chairs.

As the barista set my espresso down, he smiled, so I decided it might be appropriate to try out one of my practiced phrases.

"*Mi sono appena trasferita a Montepulciano.*" I've just moved to Montepulciano, I smiled, resisting the urge to apologize for my horrible Italian.

"*Perché?*" he asked, looking genuinely puzzled. I'd fielded this question a lot in February when I'd said I was moving here. Locals seemed bewildered that anyone would want to come and live in their town.

"*Sono scrittrice*," I told him. I'm a writer. Then I added, "*Cercavo pace.*" I was looking for peace. This didn't begin to express all the reasons why I loved Italy, but it was all I could manage. I would have liked to explain that I was supposed to be here, but I didn't know exactly how to say that, which is just as well because I probably seemed kooky enough already.

"*Ma, per sempre?*" he insisted.

Yes, I told him, I was planning to be here forever. He looked at me speculatively, then extended his hand to welcome me and introduce himself: "*Benvenuta! Sono Stefano.*"

Obviously I'd achieved some sort of new status. Despite the horrible accent and the bright orange running shoes, I was no longer a tourist. Not a local either, of course, but somehow I felt as if the first seedling of my roots had been planted. As I sipped my espresso, I chatted more with Stefano, telling him I was from New York and that I'd rented an apartment nearby. He peppered me with questions, speaking so quickly I only understood a third of what he said but I smiled saying, "*Sì,*" hoping I appeared intelligent.

As I left, I offered, "*Ci vediamo,*" which literally means "we'll see each other," but is the Italian equivalent of "see you later."

"*Volentieri,*" he replied. I had no idea what that meant, but I repeated it to myself a few times so I could remember to look it up when I get home.

Hopefully it didn't mean "*Che palle.*"

CHAPTER FOUR

THE LAY
OF THE LAND

Is it wrong to choose your town because you like the wine? I often joked this was how I settled on Montepulciano, but even without the fabulous Vino Nobile the town is famous for, I would have been in love. For me, it was like finding out a man I'd already fallen for could cook too.

To the uninitiated, Montepulciano might seem like the dozens of other hill towns in the surrounding countryside. I'd even heard tourists asking, "Now *which* town is this?" hauling out video cameras and consulting guide books, as if there were nothing to distinguish it from the others they'd so dutifully toured on their vacation. But after visiting more than my fair share of towns with an eye to living in them, I know that Montepulciano is different.

Its entrance, like many of its neighbors, is marked by an enormous stone gate, built in the ninth century. To me, the gate in itself is extraordinary. My first time walking through La Porta al Prato was like walking into a fairy tale, immediately assailed by a sense of history and the knowledge that this mammoth portal, together with the walls that surround the city, were built as protection—not only from enemy towns in an ancient age when they weren't above tossing boiling hot oil on you if you managed to break through, but also from German troops as recently as World War II. Iris Origo's diary of the latter period, which gives a first-hand account of how she shepherded dozens of children to safety in Montepulciano by walking twelve miles across the Val D'Orcia to evade the German occupying forces, is relentlessly moving and communicates the importance of the design of these edifices.

Crossing the threshold into town as a tourist and making my first passage as a resident inspired very different emotions. Tourists are typically focused on the cultural offerings or the shops, perhaps making mental notes of a wine store to visit or some local cheese to remember to buy as a gift. But as a resident, the feeling is deeper. As I passed through the archway that first morning, I was conscious that walking through this gate marked the official beginning of a new chapter of my life. And yet, any exhilaration I felt at becoming part of the tapestry of the town was immediately subsumed by the knowledge that I was an outsider. Locals gave me suspicious glances as I strolled up the main street, intent on accomplishing some of the tasks I'd appointed myself. I hadn't spoken a word, but my tendency to give a friendly smile when someone glanced at me somehow marked me as a foreigner.

There is something about this *paese* that is at once intimate without feeling claustrophobic. Sure there are the narrow cobbled streets and quaint *piazze* that you'd expect from a medieval hill town, but there is something more. In some of the other towns, I was always conscious that the locals were intent on making money from the tourists. I'd especially felt this in Assisi, which had been so tarted up after the earthquake of 1997, it was almost like being in a Disneyland version of its former self.

Montepulciano felt just the opposite. Tourists are, of course, an essential part of the livelihood of the residents, but there was also a sense of "we've been producing wine and cheese for centuries, and we'll survive just fine even if you don't buy that half-gallon of olive oil." There is no real effort by the locals to speak English to the hoards of Americans and Brits that descend each year, and by and large, you won't find menus printed in anything other than Italian. More often you'll be offered one that is hand-scribbled and nearly indecipherable. It was this authenticity that drew me to Montepulciano, the sense that these people were living real lives.

As I made my way up the street, I could barely resist poking my head into every storefront, each with alluring displays of their local products—handcrafted leather purses or olive wood that had been transformed into cutting boards and pepper mills. The tantalizing scent of cinnamon drifted from the *erboristeria*, with its rows of neatly stacked lotions and soaps on display.

At only a little after nine in the morning, most of the store owners were still setting out their goods and mopping their floors as they readied for the day. When I reached the wide limestone steps of the Chiesa di Sant'Agostino, I allowed myself to stop for a moment. The church's façade, designed by the Florentine sculptor and architect Michelozzo, captivated tourists with its gothic and Renaissance elements, including a frieze in terracotta above the doorway featuring the Madonna and Child, John the Baptist, and Saint Augustine.

But me? I loved the bells. They chimed resolutely on the hour and half hour, but when they pealed the time for Mass, they swung spiritedly like dance hall girls kicking up their skirts. These melodic bells had roused me that morning. The bells added a certain dashing quality to this triumph of the Renaissance, whose beauty was only partly diminished by the corset of scaffolding it wore while submitting to a much needed facelift.

From my perch I had the perfect vantage point to watch the activity of the street. I'd spent many hours here, writing in my journal and being part of the normal ebb and flow of life. Montepulciano is too small for a newspaper, so the town notice board serves to update residents on the latest goings-on in town. The main attractions were the birth and death notices; news of either was usually the topic of conversation for the day. I watched as an elderly woman paused in front of an announcement of someone who had just died.

Tourists, breathing heavily as they attempted to push strollers up the steep incline of the Via Gracciano nel Corso, rubbed elbows with locals doing their shopping or chatting and catching up on the latest gossip. The town is closed to tourist traffic, but occasionally a car will rumble up the hill, as will the town's little orange *autobus*, which can ferry you up to Piazza Grande if you are unable to make the climb. Engines revving as drivers try to not to roll downhill while waiting for unwitting tourists to move out of their way is a common sound.

The first few shops of the town are owned by the Ercolani family, under the name "Pulcino," which began as a nickname for the patriarch—it means "chick." From what I'd been told, they owned a lot of Montepulciano. And they were sneaky about it. Their stores all had different names and their wine was bottled under various labels as well. But inquire about work at any of these various *enoteche* and *ristoranti* and you'll soon find out that the *proprietario* (owner) is the same person for each establishment. And while the rest of Montepulciano closed down each day from one to four, Pulcino's shops remained open. They wanted the tourist business and weren't shy about soliciting it. Each *enoteca* they owned had abundant platters piled with cheese and *salumi* to sample, and if you needed a restaurant recommendation, why, they knew just the place. Tourists, confused as to why everything was closed, were lured into these shops like Snow White to her apple. They came out looking dazed, arms laden with cardboard cases of wine and bags overflowing with pecorino (aged sheep's milk cheese) wrapped *sottovuoto* (vacuum-packed) so they could take it back on the plane.

Past these tourist-magnet shops were the stores the locals actually frequented: the butcher, the cheese shop, and small grocery stores with regular customers who had established and entrenched bonds with these shopkeepers. Because I had stayed with Laura a few times, I was already familiar with some of these stores.

At the cheese shop, I knew Caterina. Thin, wiry, and in her mid-forties, her expression seemed somewhat pained when you first caught sight of her, but she was quick to smile. We'd done little more than exchange greetings on my previous trips, but she recognized me warmly, offering "*Bentornata*" to welcome me back. The glass display case was tempting, stuffed with large wheels or hunks of the local cheeses her family produced. Residents knew to come early if they wanted fresh ricotta, still warm on arrival, as Caterina only stocked six or eight containers a day.

I located the *pecorino con pepe nero* (with black peppercorns) and Caterina drew her knife around the wheel as she asked me how much she should cut.

"*Così?*" Like this?

"*Sì, perfetto,*" I told her, watching as she deftly sliced a wedge of cheese and, with practiced ease, wrapped it in paper and placed it on the scale. Pecorino was the local cheese of the region, and the sheep I'd spied from my window no doubt were busy producing the milk for this firm, tangy *formaggio*. My favorite had black peppercorns in it, but I'd tried most of them, and they were all delicious. A lunch of pecorino, a ripe pear, and a drizzle of honey was pretty much *paradiso* in my book.

My other acquaintance in town was Gabriella at the *legatoria*, a bookbinding shop that smelled richly of leather. Originally from Romania, Gabriella had lived most of her twenty-three years in Italy. She also spoke English thanks to a mom who insisted she study the language daily.

"*Ciao*, Jenny," she said immediately as I entered the shop, her dark brown eyes warm and welcoming. "You came back."

In the States, I'd always been "Jen" or "Jennifer," but from my first trip to Italy, most Italians simply called me "Jenny," and I adopted it; it made me feel youthful. We kissed hello.

"How was your travel?" she asked. "Your dog OK?" When she spoke quickly I could detect a slight stutter. My shoulders sagged with the relief of being able to speak in English as I filled her in on the last few days.

She listened, stacking some creamy note cards with prints of poppies and sunflowers, while I dallied among the journals.

The walls were lined with glossy mahogany wood shelves filled with beautiful notepads, writing paper, journals of every type, leather satchels, ink wells, and other writing implements. I tried not to think of the poor cows that gave up their lives so I could write in beautifully bound leather books.

I purchased an oversized, unlined hardcover tome. It wasn't suited to carting around, but I liked the way the thick pages felt underneath my hands and the size was perfect for stuffing in any small remembrances I might pick up along the way.

"I'll be back in soon," I promised as she wrapped up my purchase.

"You will find happiness here," Gabriella said as I left. I wasn't sure if she meant in the store or in Montepulciano, but I liked the sentiment.

Further up the cobbled street were a string of shops carrying local pottery, perfume, clothes, purses, handmade shoes, hats and scarves, copper pots and pans, and, of course, souvenirs, all sandwiched between coffee bars, grocery stores, restaurants, gelato shops, and small hotels.

And then, of course, the wine.

I've never counted the number of wine shops offering tastings of the wonderful Vino Nobile and Vino Rosso di Montepulciano, but let's just say that you could probably eat and drink at a different location for a few weeks at least. Each *enoteca* beckons with floor to ceiling bottles of wine, artfully arranged, and for a remembrance of time spent in Montepulciano, most are delighted to proffer a laminated sheet with price lists for shipping cases home.

My new bank lay halfway up the hill, as convenient for banking as it was for catching your breath. I didn't realize how steep the town is until I attempted to power up the hill en route to a specific destination. It's much more enjoyable if you have some stops to make along the way. Normally tourists could be identified by their shortness of breath. I overtook a man now, doing a mental air punch as I scooted past, only to hear wheezing and realize he was a smoker.

Laura's mom, Marisa, had introduced me around the bank in February, helping me open a checking account. I'd signed stacks of papers, with loads of tiny Italian words I couldn't understand.

"Am I signing away my first born?" I'd joked with the manager, as I blindly initialed yet another page.

"*Quasi,*" he'd replied deadpan. Almost.

I laughed. He didn't.

My mission that morning was to deposit my tiny nest egg, which I'd been assiduously collecting for many years. It wasn't much, but it would give me a cushion for a few months until I found some work. Stepping into the small futuristic pod that allowed entrance into the bank, I pushed the button, a green light came on, and the doors *whooshed* open. After they closed behind me, the ones in front of me *whooshed* open. I'm sure it was a deterrent for bank robberies because it would be really hard to try and crowd three or four robbers into the pod. Or worse yet, to be holding your bag of loot and then get trapped inside when the doors locked down. It was like a life-sized version one of those pneumatic containers that banks use in drive-through lanes to shuttle your money back and forth.

In stark contrast to the futuristic pod, the inside of the bank felt old-fashioned with no glass windows separating customers from the tellers; they sat behind tall wooden desks, were friendly, and knew everyone on sight. I half-expected a man holding a ledger and wearing a green visor to emerge from the back and flash me a wink and a smile to assure me he'd just put my money in the safe.

There was only one person ahead of me, an old woman explaining about some hard times with her husband. Her banking seemed to be completed, but she needed an ear, and the teller, Daniela, was patient. Daniela is one of those extraordinarily pretty Italian girls you want to hate but because she's so nice, you can't help but like her. I met her on my last visit. She gave me a wave and an "I'll only be another minute" look while she talked to the woman.

When it was my turn, I told Daniela I needed to make a deposit. There would be no deposit slips to fill out—Daniela knew who I was, as she knew all of the customers, so I just told her what I needed. She clicked away at her computer, completed the transaction, printed out my receipt, I signed it, and I was done. After the cattle-like experience of big city banking, this felt both cozy and alien.

✦　　✦　　✦

Chopped onion sizzled as it met hot oil in a waiting pot. On its heels followed carrot, celery, and parsley. I also added some garlic. Although the Tuscans didn't seem to put garlic in all of their recipes, my grandmother had always used it liberally in her cooking. It's what makes us spicy Sicilians, I thought as I sipped my glass of Vino Nobile, letting the subtle flavors of cherry and wild berries settle on my tongue.

Flush with the satisfaction of my morning outings, I'd then successfully navigated the supermarket outside the walls of the town. I'd secured vegetables, *vitello e maiale macinato* (ground veal and pork) for the ragù, tomatoes, bread, wine, and other ingredients I needed to make my first official dinner. I'd been slightly stymied by the pasta aisle. Why are there so many shapes? And how could you ever remember what pasta went with what sauce? I knew this was important to Italians based on a friend's story about once using the wrong-sized spaghetti; it became the main topic of dinner conversation. Marisa had also explained to me that you'd never use the local *pici* pasta to make a carbonara, even though it looks like a fatter version of spaghetti.

"*Pici* wants a ragù," she told me. "Or an *aglione*." (This is a spicy tomato sauce, one Tuscan dish in which garlic is used abundantly and which takes its name from *aglio*, the Italian word for garlic.)

Yes, the pasta aisle was quite confusing, so in the end I grabbed multiple packages of different shapes and sizes to cover my bases.

Now, as I prepared my ragù, I added the ground veal and pork and two sausages squeezed out of their casings. Mine wouldn't have Marisa's special ingredient of chicken livers, but it would still be tasty. I set the table with a pretty pink-checked cloth and arranged newly bought yellow gerbera daisies in a skinny glass jug.

At least now we had light in the chandelier. I'd taken Cinder with me in the afternoon to find a hardware store and to see about getting Internet service. As we'd explored I felt the eyes of the town upon us, taking our measure. Walking the tree-lined streets, I became aware that I literally didn't fit in with the smaller-statured Tuscans. The trees were all trimmed to a height below my five feet nine inches, which necessitated ducking my head every time I passed under them. As for Cinder, I might have had a dancing bear on the end of the leash rather than a dog, so curious were the locals. People stopped me, wondering about her breed, "*Che razza è?*"

"Weimaraner" didn't seem to make much sense to them so I added "*di Germania*" and they'd nod like that made it all quite clear. Big dogs in Italy were usually hunting dogs, and they were kept to their yards and gardens where they could make a big show of barking at every passerby. People obviously weren't prepared for the sight of an eighty-pound Weimaraner docilely strolling the streets. I hadn't brought her with me to *centro* because it was quite the *disgrazia* for your dog to poop on the street there ... even if you had every intention of cleaning it up. After nine years in New York and loads of encouragement, Cinder now was a veteran street pooper, so I was pretty confident if I brought her with me and willed her not to poop, she'd pick that moment to do a *grande* one in the main square.

Although my shop visits went smoothly enough when I browsed, they inevitably turned arduous when there was something I needed but couldn't find. My encounter with the man at the Internet store ended up being more painfully slow than the speed of the 3G key he finally gave me to log on to the web.

But the most frustrating experience was at the hardware store.

The stout woman with a helmet of spray-starched gray curls who owned the store was initially patient with me as I tried to find the correct lightbulbs for the living room chandelier. I'd made a note that the word for lightbulb was *lampadina* but hadn't taken into consideration all of the different varieties with enough sub-nomenclature to give me flashbacks of biology class. She rooted around all sorts of electrical equipment, plugs and cords, digging into drawers, bringing forth every bulb she had. I kept repeating, "*Più piccola*," which I was pretty confident meant "a little smaller," all the while doing my best imitation of a chandelier hanging from the ceiling. She finally located what I needed, and we exchanged sighs of relief. I was pleased I'd been able to communicate my needs, albeit awkwardly, so as I paid I attempted a little conversation to let her know I'd moved here permanently. She immediately suggested I enroll at the language school in town. "Before you come back" was unspoken but implied. I departed with lightbulbs and lower self-esteem.

But as the ragù simmered and I sipped my wine, I felt better. I added some wine to the pot, then used my newly procured Internet to Skype Cheryl and then Will. When Cheryl came on the screen, sitting behind her desk, wearing her lawyer's suit and her usual mask of stress, tears pricked my eyes. I succeeded in making her laugh as I filled her in on my day's adventure.

"I just can't believe your table wine is Vino Nobile," she said wistfully, staring at my glass. "It really isn't fair."

"Don't worry," I told her. "There will still be plenty when you come to visit."

Will, as always, was more interested in my love life. "Who are you cooking for?" he'd demanded. "Have you found a man already?"

I laughed. "Don't worry, there will still be plenty here when you come to visit."

I felt more centered after the calls. My tiny urban family was still there, even if they were far away. I stirred the sauce, waiting to add the tomatoes until the alcohol from the wine had evaporated. I thought about Will's words. He knew me too well. I had purposely avoided any serious romantic entanglements during my time in New York, instead trying to repair the damage that had been done to my heart years earlier. But whenever I was in Italy, my resolve weakened, and I felt drawn to these passionate men whose eyes left nothing unsaid.

I added some freshly chopped basil to the ragù and left it to simmer. Like all things worth waiting for, it needed time.

CHAPTER FIVE

I MIEI VICINI

"*Ciaorigo!*"

My neighbor Marinella's voice carried through the open sliver of my window, which was open not because of a sudden heat wave, but rather because with the damp air outside, my house had developed a distinctly unsexy odor of *eau de Cinder*. Mornings persisted in their ominous gray drizzle, and we were two days from May. Every time I'd traveled to Italy no matter what season, I'd only ever encountered sunshine and perhaps one day of precipitation. I vaguely remembered a rain shower in Capri, a brief flurry of snow in Tuscany. But this day-after-day gloom was unusual, and it didn't help me feel settled. The frozen tiles of my apartment at times seemed to be conspiring to suck the life, and the confidence, right out of me.

When I heard Marinella's call again, I peered through the *tendine*, crocheted curtains, that all the windows in town seemed to sport, to see what she was doing. We'd met briefly, and I'd heard her many times over the last couple of days. This was partly because after my morning errands I'd spent much of my days at home. I hadn't made any friends yet, and other than a few hours here and there sitting in town and writing in my journal or grabbing a coffee at the bar, I'd felt shy about venturing out on my own. My passing acquaintances from vacation visits didn't seem very enthusiastic about chatting with me, but I didn't blame them. I couldn't speak proper Italian! My vocabulary was like that of a four-year-old. I was so slow and awkward in forming sentences that one shop owner asked me to speak in English—particularly painful because she knew only five words of English herself. Apparently it was just too gruesome to listen to me butcher the lovely and melodic language that is Italian. And maybe I was paranoid, but it seemed that every time I offered my cheery "*Ci vediamo*" when I departed a store, the shopkeepers saw it as some sort of threat. "*For the love of God, why does she keep saying we'll see each other? How long did she say she's staying in town?*"

And so I'd become increasingly timid about speaking. Which meant I wasn't practicing. And that meant I wasn't likely to improve any time soon. I knew that if I couldn't speak properly, I was going to have a really hard time finding work. Or making friends. Or doing anything.

But I'm also quite stubborn, so I just kept doing what I was doing and hoping that my Italian would somehow magically get better.

I believe this is the "Head in the Sand" stage of expatdom.

Laura hadn't come to see me, but Marisa had stopped in the day before for about thirty seconds with two boxes of my things and a five-liter drum of olive oil. I was so happy to see her I almost cried. We'd had such an enjoyable visit in February, I'd imagined I'd be spending most of my time with them. My vision of my "welcome" had included their descending on my doorstep with outstretched arms and whisking me away for dinner with the family. But aside from a few brief texts from Laura apologizing and telling me how busy they were at the agriturismo, there had been nothing. I'd failed to take into consideration that they worked all day running the farm and just didn't have time for social chats. Plus, since I didn't have a car, I had no way of getting out to see them.

At least you're in Tuscany. For the past few days, anytime I'd encounter a difficult situation, like stern lightbulb-wielding store owners, I'd repeat that to myself. It was my Italian version of the fortune cookie game in which you read your fortune out loud, adding "in bed" at the end. "You will find true happiness . . . in bed." I'd just modified it to "in Tuscany." Well, at least the day is crap . . . in Tuscany. At least you have no friends and can't speak the language . . . in Tuscany.

I'd also turned to voyeurism as a means of passing the time, watching the people on my street as if they were characters in a play. Marinella had a large house, the biggest on the block. Set apart from the rest, it boasted a pretty garden with loads of flowers, trees, and shrubs in a color scheme of bright pinks, reds, and purples. Everything seemed to be planted haphazardly in a "this is pretty, I'll put it here" kind of way, but somehow it worked. Protecting the house from behind the confines of a tall, jasmine-covered fence was a large black and white unneutered dog named Ozzy.

Marinella's "*Ciaorigo!*" was directed at the old man who lived next to me—not the neighbors with the splashy orange kitchen; they were a beautiful young couple I hadn't met yet, but I'd heard some energetic retching from their bathroom window, and I'd glimpsed them hugging and kissing as they cooked their evening meal. Were they newlyweds? Possibly pregnant?

The man who lived on the far side of me was Alrigo, but when Marinella greeted him it always sounded like one word. His typical response to her "*Ciaorigo!*" was "*Aooo!*" It kind of reminded me of the sound you'd make if you'd just stubbed your toe. Alrigo was tall and thin with weathered skin like a deeply tanned rhinoceros and spoke of a lifetime of laboring outside. Eighty if he was a day, he wore the same uniform without fail: green camouflage pants, green sweater, and black Nike sneakers that seemed a size too big. Sometimes he added an old khaki-colored cap for variety.

Alrigo drove one of the three-wheeled farm trucks that snaked along Tuscan roads at about ten miles an hour called an Ape (pronounced AH-peh), which means honeybee; the noise they make sounds much like the buzzing of a bee. They're made by Piaggio, the same company that makes the Vespa or "wasp." Every morning at 7:30 sharp, Alrigo motored away, returning home for lunch, his truck packed with skinny pieces of firewood. Sometimes he'd have a demijohn of wine beside him. Long before the noisy engine sputtered up the street, the keen ears on his beagle mix would prick, and he'd bark and whine in anticipation. The dog lived in a shed, from which he'd emerge through a makeshift pen to bark at passersby. I called him "Zitto" because Alrigo's yells of "*Stai zitto!*" (Be quiet!) would echo down the street whenever the dog began his incessant barking. Despite his barking spurts, Zitto appeared sweet enough, and he and Alrigo seemed to be good companions, once you got over the whole dog-has-to-sleep-in-a-shed-and-spends-his-days-in-a-five-foot-by-three-foot-pen thing. Some mornings I'd see Alrigo, leaning on a walking stick to keep his balance, taking Zitto on slow walks down the mountain. Then there were the things that I really, really didn't want to know. Like the fact that Alrigo, or one of my other elderly neighbors who lived across from me, liked to masturbate in the afternoon. Nearly every day at the same time the noise of some enthusiastic grunting wafted into my apartment. I'd taken to turning up the volume on my television at that hour, preferring to listen to a dubbed version of *Murder She Wrote*. Most of the old people had their televisions cranked way up during pranzo anyway. I was beginning to think the median age on my block might be just shy of Methuselah.

During one of my midday strolls with Cinder, Ozzy, his gate open, wandered into the parking area as Marinella set out food for some cats. Ozzy wasted no time in racing over to sniff Cinder.

"*Ciao*, Jennifer," Marinella called. She smiled as she approached, then called a greeting to one of our other neighbors, Ada, the town seamstress who peered curiously out her window. Marinella's voice was melodic and reminded me of the birds I so liked hearing each morning. Taller than the average Italian woman, Marinella regarded everyone with kind brown eyes, and her movements were spare and purposeful. We'd exchanged the preliminaries during our first encounters, but I could tell she wanted to know more. Indeed, she'd asked a lot of questions, but my vocabulary hadn't allowed me to give her the information she needed. "*Piano, piano,*" she'd consoled when I apologized for my lack of proficiency. Little by little.

From my perch on the splintered wooden bench in the parking area, I could watch the tourists trek up the wide stone steps, a shortcut to and from the public parking. One day when a British couple came huffing and puffing up the steps, pausing to take a photo of the "quaint laundry" hanging out our windows, I startled them with my English. "I wouldn't take any photos of mine," I teased. "I've just moved here, and I don't think I'm doing it right."

Truth be told, laundry was a nightmare. My washing machine, with the unlikely brand name of Candy, may have sweetly served a mid-century housewife but now was so ancient that all it had left to offer was the dyspeptic sound of water trickling in and out and the vague memory of a more vigorous time. I'd learned I needed to manually spin the inner metal cylinder a few times during the two-hour cycle if I wanted all of the clothes to get wet, and mostly ended up reaching in to hand wash them myself. The process lent new meaning to the word *agitation.*

Then there was the drying. Prior to my move, my only experience with hanging anything outside to dry was an occasional beach towel flung over a hotel railing on vacation. In my dreams of Tuscany, I imagined this sort of back-to-basics thing would be fun. But let me disabuse anyone of that notion. Wrestling sopping wet duvet covers onto thin wire laundry cords perched outside the window was never, not for one moment, fun. Dangerous? Often. Time-consuming? Definitely. Challenging? Yes. But fun? Not so much.

Unlike Marinella, whose laundry lines were at ground level in her yard, I had to hang my entire torso out the window to reach mine. While my neighbors' lines squeaked confidently as they clipped on their sheets, pillowcases, and yes, even their underwear, mine instead groaned disapprovingly as I failed to master the requisite two-inch border over the line that everyone seemed to do with ease. How did they achieve such perfection without falling out the window? Success for me was draping the clothes over the line without tumbling headlong into the gravel below.

But as annoying as this whole process was, all was forgiven once the clothes were dried. The Tuscan sun and wind worked their magical alchemy, and the clothes off the line became crisp, fragrant, and miraculously free of dog hair. Each time I pulled my laundry in, I was a new mother—so pleased with the glorious result of my labor, I'd happily forget the pain and suffering involved.

Today Marinella followed my gaze to the laundry as she drew near, the corner of her mouth betraying a twist of amusement.

"*Che caldo,*" she said. It was partly sunny, maybe sixty-five degrees and in no way hot, but I was noticing it was customary to begin casual conversations with either "*Che freddo*" (how cold it was) or "*Che caldo*" (how hot it was). The trick was to say it in a very dramatic tone that somehow lent importance and gravity to an otherwise trivial statement. Marinella usually added a "*Madonnina!*" at the end of hers. At first, I tried to respond with something like "*Sì, ma è una bella giornata,*" (yes, but it's a beautiful day) until I realized my job was to simply agree and move on.

"*Sì, caldo,*" I smiled. Marinella was holding the small plastic container she used to feed the cats. I watched as she placed the kitty kibble on the low stone wall, explaining that the five cats were hers.

"My youngest son is a veterinarian, so guess who ends up with all the abandoned animals?" she told me in Italian. "That's how I ended up with that hairy beast, too," she chuckled, nodding toward Ozzy, who was at the moment trying to figure out a way to initiate a *Mrs. Robinson*-style seduction scene with my old girl. Cinder planted her haunches and sat primly at my feet. Denied.

As she chatted about her two sons, I realized that Marinella is what is known here as a "*mammina.*" It's an affectionate term used by men who rely on their mothers for everything. Though in their thirties, both sons still lived at home, returning each afternoon for pranzo without fail, their cars kicking up gravel as they zoomed into the parking area so as to arrive to the table precisely at one. On the positive side, at least there was a veterinarian living within shouting distance in case of emergency, even if he wasn't yet ready to leave the nest.

Marinella had been slowly pumping me for information on my marital status, my job, and my plans for the future.

"*Quanti anni hai?*" she asked that day as she fed the cats, curious about my age. I knew it was just a matter of time.

The corners of her mouth dropped when I revealed my thirty-eight years. The words "*troppo vecchia*" flashed in neon above her head. Too old. Maybe she'd had me in mind as a wife for the vet? I imagined myself thirty years from now, cooking lunch each day for my husband and two grown sons, loaded down with stray cats and abandoned dogs. Marinella made a little more chit-chat, patted an orange kitty called Teo, and then headed back into her house.

Italians have a strange relationship with animals. On the surface they seem to adore them. They rush over to shower dogs with attention, they allow them in shops and cafes, they welcome them on trains, but then in summer many go on vacation and abandon their pets on the side of the road. And I don't mean fifty or even a hundred. I mean over 300,000 cats and dogs each year. I don't get it. I can't even imagine booking my summer vacation to the beach and then just dropping Cinder off on the side of the highway. "*If you start walking now, and you don't get killed by a car, we should both get back to the house around the same time. Buona fortuna.*"

I asked Marinella why so many pets were abandoned in this manner, and she said simply because people were *cattiva*, or wicked. It was such an issue that before summer even began there were a spate of public service announcements with Italian celebrities who had rescued strays entreating people not to dump their animals.

Cinder had experienced the adoration side of this equation at our bar. Serena, Stefano's wife, loved dogs and when I hesitated outside one morning, she told me it was OK to bring Cinder in. The next thing I knew, Serena was bringing out a thick wad of prosciutto, kneeling to offer it to Cinder with a grin. For Cinder, it was love at first sight . . . and she thought Serena was pretty great too. Now, even on days when I didn't want to stop by the bar, we stopped by the bar. It was that or face the inevitable test of sheer will-power and brute strength as Cinder employed the tried and true "I'll pull your arm off" maneuver to get her way. I had to hand it to her: for an old girl, Cinder was pretty darn strong.

Now that I'd become a frequent customer at the bar, Serena and I were getting to know one another. I sipped espresso while Serena grilled me on life in the United States, pushing her curly dark brown hair from her face every few moments, an expression of intensity on her face that often made her appear far older than her thirty years. But her countenance changed when she smiled, the furrow of her brow dissolving into a woman surprisingly warm, pretty, and youthful.

Serena loved all things American, especially New York, and most of our conversations consisted of her trying to talk me out of staying in Montepulciano and heading back to La Grande Mela (The Big Apple).

"It is possible to find work in New York?" she attempted in tentative English. She'd taken some classes and had spent a little time in the States, but like me and my Italian, she was self-conscious about the way she sounded. I studied the bags under Serena's bright blue eyes, which until now I'd attributed to her incredible commitment to the bar. She and Stefano had just opened the place a few months prior, so I couldn't imagine they were ready to pack it in and move on. But now I wondered if maybe there was something else prompting these specific questions about living in New York. Maybe Serena was planning a move on her own? I didn't know her well enough to pry into her personal life.

"Maybe one night we can go for a pizza," she said one day as I was leaving. "I would like to introduce you to some of my friends."

"That would be great," I told her, excited at the prospect of making new acquaintances. Meeting Serena and having a place to go each day had definitely helped me feel more connected. I hoped that one day I would be able to repay her kindness.

CHAPTER SIX

MARKET DAY

Every Italian town has a designated market day and Montepulciano's is Thursday. If you enjoy the thrill of the hunt, bargaining for discounted prices, and returning home with loads of things you didn't really need but couldn't resist, then you need to experience an Italian market day. Every week vendors from neighboring towns come to sell clothes, plants, housewares, gardening supplies, rugs, fabrics, shoes, luggage and purses, rattan, wicker, even live chickens, all in the open air. Tables are laden with seasonal produce: apples, melons, apricots, berries, arugula, leeks, zucchini flowers, cabbage, tomatoes; as well as local cheeses, jams, candies, *salumi*, fish, eggs, roasted chicken and pork—even early in the morning the smells emanating from the roasted meats are obscenely seductive.

A weekly ritual for most residents (both for shopping and for catching up with neighbors) and a must-see for visitors, Montepulciano's market overwhelmed me with the quantity of amazing things you could find at reasonable prices during my first visit—so much so that I ended up having to buy another suitcase just to pack all of my treasures for the trip home.

As the gray skies of April burned away, May brought sunshine and breezy warm weather. The green hills were afire with vibrant Tuscan red poppies, and I felt energized as I tossed on jeans and a long-sleeved T-shirt, preparing to head down to the market. At the last moment I wrapped a long champagne-pink scarf around my neck in attempt to dress up my outfit a bit.

Forget everything you've heard about Italian fashion. It doesn't apply in this part of Tuscany. Women don't prance around Montepulciano in killer heels, looking like they've just stepped off a Milan runway. Jeans, flip flops, shorts, basically all of the things I had thought were verboten were on full display by merchants and locals. Only at night do you ever see a few women dressed to the nines. The acquaintances I'd made were usually in jeans and T-shirts, so I fit right in. My neighborhood in New York was one that a friend liked to call "aggressively unfashionable," and for someone like me, whose wardrobe consisted of a lot of clothes suitable for rolling around with dogs in the park, not having to worry about my lack of stylish clothing was a relief.

Marinella had mentioned exploring the market together, but after hanging about for a few moments with no sign of her, I decided to take Cinder and strike out on my own since most vendors set up by eight and began breaking down by lunchtime.

Montepulciano's market isn't in the historic section, but is down the hill past the supermarket. The area designated for the market is basically the overflow parking lot for the town's bus station. In summer, campers clutter the space to park their trailers for overnights. But not on Thursday.

Cinder and I did a quick loop around to all of the vendors. An old woman sitting stoically behind an unadorned table selling fresh ricotta. Caravans full of fabrics, housewares, and handmade linens being unloaded. Men using long poles to hang blouses, purses, and bathmats on the awnings of their trailers. I spied a *fruttivendolo*, a fruit and vegetable vendor, set apart from the others and headed that way, away from the forming lines. I could never seem to construct coherent sentences when there was a group of people queuing behind me, impatient. A delicious *profumo* from the strawberries floated in the air, and I asked the two young men behind the table for a *cestino*—I'd heard the woman in front of me do the same, so I hoped it was a real word. I breathed a sigh of relief when I was handed a small basket of ruby-red strawberries. My knowledge of metric measurements was abysmal, but I did remember that a half-kilo is about one pound. I'd found this out the hard way at the grocery store when I'd ordered a kilo of prosciutto and ended up with over two pounds of cured ham! That was one lesson Cinder didn't mind.

As I meandered through the market, I succeeded in getting a pound of onions, a *mazzo* (bunch) of asparagus, and four apples. When all else failed, I held up my fingers to express amounts. I was getting better with the money, and I fished around for the right change, earning a nod of approval from the vendor. In New York, you were likely to get stoned if you even reached for a change purse in a transaction, but the Italians loved exact change. It wasn't unusual for people to take an extra minute or two to pull together the correct amount; some of the town elders, trusting souls that they were, would even proffer a handful for the vendor to count it out. The "*Brava!*" I received after each transaction was like my own personal standing ovation. No longer was I a visitor who merely plunked down my fifty-euro note just withdrawn from the *bancomat* (ATM), using up all the vendor's change. It was a small accomplishment but satisfying nonetheless.

My next task was rug shopping since Luciana had cleaned out the apartment of any and all floor accessories, and I gravitated toward a vendor with a display of colorful area rugs suspended on his trailer and laid over long tables. All types of rugs in every size imaginable overlapped one another. Wild prints, geometric designs, and solids as well as luxuriously patterned oriental rugs. While it wasn't considered good form to negotiate with the food vendors, the other vendors expected it; it was part of the customary exchange. An oriental rug in deep sage shot with threads of black and rose caught my eye.

"*Quanto costa?*" I asked, pointing to the one I liked.

The vendor pulled the rug closer for my inspection. "*Duecento.*"

My face fell. Two hundred euros was way over my budget. That was nearly two hundred and fifty dollars!

"OK, *grazie.*" I began to walk away, but the fast-talking vendor thought I was being coy and lowered the price on it three times in the next five minutes.

"*Bello,*" I told him. "*Torno senza il mio cane.*" I'll come back without my dog.

He gave me the "Sure, I've heard that one before" look, then in desperation dropped the price again. His face looked pained. "*Signorina, non posso fare di più.*" I can't do any more.

"*Torno,*" I assured him, dragging Cinder away. I would come back later and buy the rug now that it was in my price range. My first foray into market bargaining had been a success; it made no difference to my psyche that I hadn't actually been trying to get a better price. I really was just going to take my dog home and come back. It felt like one step closer to becoming a part of the town, though, and that's all that mattered.

Before I could even head toward the exit, Cinder pulled me over to the truck selling *porchetta,* savory roasted pork with (at times) an overly salty stuffing. I caught sight of the pig's head positioned next to the roasted pork body and hesitated. It seemed to be staring balefully in my direction. But the aroma of the roasted meat was too tantalizing to resist so I allowed Cinder to lead me toward the end of the already long line. Some people chatted as they waited for a *panino* with *porchetta* to munch on while browsing the market. I studiously avoided eye contact with the pig.

When it was our turn, Cinder couldn't contain herself and jumped up on the side of the truck, barking sharply in her excitement. Thankfully the truck was too high for her to reach the pig's head. I could just see her dashing through the aisles dragging it by an ear. The brawny man wielding a huge knife who was serving me laughed.

"*Per due?*" he asked. For two?

"*Sempre,*" I told him, smiling ruefully. Always.

He then waved his knife toward two pieces of pork, a full-fat version, plump and scrumptious and one that was *magra,* or lean.

"*Magra, per favore,*" I told him, then collected our lunch. I always find it easier to be virtuous in the morning.

Circling back out of the market so I could drop off Cinder and come back for the rug, I spotted Luciana, our landlady. She kept a safe distance from Cinder, yelling a gravelly, "*Tutto a posto?*"

"*Sì, tutto a posto!*" Everything was fine at the apartment—after all, I didn't know how to say, "Except for Cinder scratching some of the plaster off the wall near the front door the first few times I left her alone." I'd strategically positioned a plant there to cover her damage. Our little secret, Cinder.

"*Lunedì, andiamo al' avvocato,*" she reminded me. "*Alle tre. Hai capito?*"

Yes, I understood, and I tried to arrange my face into a semblance of something other than dismay. Not only did I not want to spend any quality time with Luciana on Monday, but I wasn't likely to understand much of what the lawyer was saying anyway. Unfortunately, it was an unavoidable step in finishing my lease.

"*Ho capito,*" I told her. I was saved from further conversation when Marinella spotted me and rushed over, waving as best she could with her arms full of bags. She wore a vibrant cardigan in the color of spring irises and had a creamy silk scarf knotted at her neck, and she'd taken the time to put on eye makeup. She looked quite pretty and definitely less mom-like. She and Luciana greeted each other stiffly; it seemed that they weren't exactly friends, which somehow made me like my neighbor even more.

As Luciana departed, Marinella turned her attention to me, eyeing my bags of fruit. "You're doing the shopping? Which vendor did you go to?"

I pointed to the far side, and she shook her head mournfully.

"*Troppo costoso.*" I half-expected her to say "*Disgrazia*" and spit, a product of too many Italian movies on my part, no doubt.

Clutching my arm, she led me to a section of the market out of the main loop, slightly to the right where just a few vendors set up. Apparently this was where the locals shopped.

"This is Salvatore," she said, gesturing to a tall, handsome man who stood in front of a mountain of oranges. He was surrounded on three sides by tables laden with apples, apricots, strawberries, asparagus, artichokes, zucchini, tomatoes, and new spring greens. In the morning sunlight, his brown hair glinted with silver, I guessed he was probably mid- to late forties.

"*Amore!*" he called to Marinella, then grinned. Wolfishly. He loped around the tables so he could hug me too, holding my gaze for a moment, his eyes a mercurial shade of blue and silver. Apparently Salvatore was a bit of a flirt.

Unlike the other produce vendors where you must ask for what you want, Salvatore had blue plastic bags available and allowed his customers to select their own fruit and vegetables—and even touch them, which is often a big no-

no with produce both at outdoor markets and in supermarkets. I'd just bought apples, but Marinella insisted that Salvatore's were the best, so I grabbed a few more. I trailed Marinella as she stuffed asparagus, oranges, ripe red tomatoes, and more into her bags and into mine.

My eyes followed Salvatore as he laughed and joked with his clients. A cigarette pinched between two fingers, he smoked, placed bags of fruit on the scale, called out totals, and put money in a small metal cash box, offering handfuls of *odori*—carrots, celery, and parsley—to those who wanted it, all without losing a beat. Most of his clients seemed to be women. I smiled as an older woman giggled girlishly when he called her "*signorina*." Perhaps this explained Marinella's makeup this morning?

When we approached with our bags, Salvatore flicked his cigarette to the ground and pulled a penknife from the pocket of his jeans. He ran his hands over the pile of apricots, finding one he liked, and then sliced the ripe fruit in two. He offered one half to Marinella and the other to me.

"Try," he ordered. "Salvatore's fruit is the best." Another grin. Definitely *come un lupo*, I thought. Like a wolf.

I sank my teeth into the orange flesh, not caring that juice was dribbling down my chin as I popped the rest into my mouth. "*Buona*," I told him, as he nodded approvingly. There was something so sexy and carnal about him that I felt myself being pulled in.

"How long are you staying in Italy?" Salvatore asked as Marinella and I gathered our bags. He had a deep booming voice, and his Italian was hard for me to understand. I didn't recognize the accent, but it was definitely not *toscano*.

"I'm here for good." He winked and seemed about to say something else when Marinella grabbed me by the arm and told him goodbye.

"*Alla prossima settimana*," I called as she dragged me away.

"He's married," she said firmly as we headed out of the market. "The wife is in Sicily." Hmm. I looked back at Salvatore who caught my eye and flashed me one last grin. I was sure Marinella assumed that would be the end of the matter, but something told me it wasn't.

CHAPTER SEVEN

BECOMING ITALIAN

I sat outside the *comune* waiting for it to open, pulling my sweater more tightly around me as the ever-present wind that whistled merrily through the piazza made the morning chilly despite the strong sun in the sky. Piazza Grande is the main square of Montepulciano but unlike other towns where the main piazza is in the center of town, here it's at the top. And they don't make it easy to get there. About three-quarters up the hill, you reach a fork in the road with confusing signs insisting that both directions lead to Piazza Grande. The route to the left is a scenic stroll, providing a spectacular view of the countryside, the Basilica of San Biagio, and the town's fortress (newly renovated, it will soon serve as the home of the Consortium of Vino Nobile) before it circles around to Piazza Grande.

Veer right and almost straight up and the reward for summiting the hill will be to reach the main square in a more direct manner. The town's museum, library, *duomo*, and local government are all here, and Piazza Grande also hosts most of the yearly wine tasting, art, and musical festivals.

The *comune*'s stone building, the financial and political heart of the town, was built in the fourteenth century, complete with a medieval tower. In its offices, residents can do everything from registering to get married to filing a complaint against a neighbor to my objective of the day—requesting residency. This was the next step in a process I'd started over three years before: becoming an Italian citizen.

It sounded simple enough. If you had Italian ancestors, you could request dual Italian citizenship. But once I began the process, I realized there were painfully specific requirements to show that no one in my family chain had renounced their Italian citizenship. Not to mention the hard part: trying to locate original documents. I'd spent these last three years requesting birth and marriage certificates from tiny *comuni* in Sicily where my ancestors had lived before their emigration to the States.

I'd visited the *comune* in Montepulciano briefly in February before my move and had spent one of the most uncomfortable hours of my life trying to explain my mission to the two women who handled the residency applications for the city.

They were an incongruous pair. Rosanna resembled an aging beauty queen with pendulous breasts stuffed into a tight T-shirt, while Vania, with her super-comfy casual wear, had the look of a camp counselor and seemed ready for a pickup game of *calcio* if the need should arise. Neither spoke English, and although I'd come with an explanatory script, they still weren't really sure what I was talking about or what I was attempting to do. When I'd told the Italian Consulate in New York I was moving to Italy and couldn't wait until October for my appointment with them, they instructed me to apply directly in the *comune* of the town I'd chosen.

Obviously that plan had a few kinks in it.

I'd finally resorted to calling Laura, interrupting her appointment with the baker making her wedding cake to plead for her to explain my situation. I think the women were as relieved, if not more than I was, when she got on the phone.

After speaking with Laura, Vania, the camp counselor, who was definitely the more patient of the two, led me into a small office overflowing with colorful, fat binders, which no doubt contained all of Montepulciano's official records. The place didn't seem to be automated judging by the bulky desktop computers, circa 1985. Vania looked over all of my original documents and found them to be in order. I was only missing one thing to start the citizenship process. I left with instructions on what to do when I returned permanently.

And now, several months later, I arrived at the next step: applying for citizenship. Though I was still waiting on that one document, I was hoping we could at least start the application.

When the doors opened, all the employees looked stressed. They rushed down the cavernous hall, ducking in and out of offices, calling out tasks to be done. I heard the words *new moon* more than once and realized everyone was talking about the *Twilight* sequel, which was about to begin filming here. They couldn't have picked a better spot since Montepulciano already looked like a town right out of central casting. I'd glimpsed loads of expectant teenagers picking up information sheets at the *tabaccheria* so they could be extras in the new vampire movie.

Scanning the offices, I saw no sign of Vania or Rosanna. Marinella had mentioned that her older son, Lorenzo, worked for the *comune*, and I glanced around trying to spot his bald head. Maybe I could prevail upon him for some help, although, unlike his brother the vet who actually said hello to me, Lorenzo usually seemed intent on ignoring me.

I hesitated outside the office for a minute before I spotted Vania rushing down the hall from another room with her arms stacked with papers and a pair of running shoes on, which I could tell she wished were a pair of skates. Her head nod in my direction told me she remembered me. But she was warm and showed no sign of impatience, despite being obviously overwhelmed. She typed on her computer for a few minutes as I kept silent. Then she finally lifted her head to address me.

"We can't start the citizenship application until you get that last document, but your residency is finalized. *Tutto a posto.* Just come back when you receive the document, and we'll get the rest underway."

I beamed, hardly able to contain my excitement. *Tutto a posto?* Everything was in place. It almost seemed too easy. I sent a text to Laura:

Tutto a posto con la mia residenza. Sono ufficiale! Celebriamo!

Everything is OK with my residency. I'm official! Let's celebrate!

CHAPTER EIGHT

LAVORO?

With my residency *tutto a posto*, I figured I'd find some work in a restaurant or a shop without much difficulty, so I'd given myself a couple of weeks to get acclimated and have a little vacation before tourist season would really heat up.

The days began to warm and before I knew it May was almost over. Tufts of white fluff from the poplar trees blew around making the town seem sprinkled with cotton candy, calling to mind that wonderful lunch with a friend in San Gimignano years before.

Yes, this was the Tuscany I was hoping for.

One morning as the sun was still yawning awake, Cinder and I strolled through the quiet streets toward the bar. The freshly baked, still-warm pastries arrived from the *forno* (bakery) at 6:30 a.m.; we were there shortly thereafter. Unlike in the States where you might leisurely enjoy your brioche with a cup of coffee, here the ritual was a little different.

"*Buongiorno,*" Serena called sleepily from behind the bar as she tamped coffee into the espresso machine for a farmer awaiting his morning brew. I eyed the glass case of pastries, dithering as I did each morning. Chocolate-filled or apricot *marmellata*?

Serena gathered her tongs, then wrapped my decadent chocolate-filled choice in a napkin. "*Caffè macchiato?*" she asked.

"*Sì, grazie.*" I bit into the flaky brioche. The custom was to eat standing up, elbow to elbow with other regulars, becoming covered with flecks of buttery pastry and dollops of filling. Cinder stood by, kindly performing clean-up duty for anyone within range of her leash. When I was about halfway through with the pastry, Serena prepared my coffee. I usually had an espresso with a tiny dollop of foamy milk. Stained, they called it. *Macchiato.*

Was there a more delightful way to start the day?

I began my job hunt slowly, a few places each day. The first stops were all *completo* but people obligingly took my number and promised to call if anything opened up. Just to be safe, I began drafting a flyer offering English lessons.

While on my daily search, I made a point of stopping into Caterina's cheese shop as well as Gabriella's bookbinder shop. My refrigerator overflowed with varieties of pecorino at this point, but making small purchases at each store afforded me a chance to speak a little. Very little. As with everyone I met on my daily sojourns, Gabriella and Caterina had assumed I was a rich American. They were surprised to learn that I was renting an apartment and was actually trying to find work. I tried to be clear about this point as I didn't want anyone to think I was just here on a lark with loads of money to burn. When people heard that I was a writer, they immediately mentioned *Under the Tuscan Sun.* I quickly discovered that many Tuscans did not think highly of the book or its author Frances Mayes, most of those I spoke to referring to her as "*quella donna.*" That woman. They felt she'd unfairly stereotyped the Tuscan people in the book. And they really disliked the movie. A lot of the Cortona scenes had been shot in Montepulciano, and they took umbrage at how Italians were portrayed as archetypes and not as true people. "*Non ci siamo,*" Caterina told me, meaning they didn't agree with the portrayal at all.

Caterina was always keen to learn more about my family, and my Italian ancestry had her declaring to a customer one day, "We're adopting her." She'd clucked sympathetically when I shared with her the story of my grandmother's brother who had gotten on the wrong side of the Mafia and had been killed in a brutal scene right out of the *Godfather* saga, and that my grandmother had never been quite the same after his death.

Each day when I saw Gabriella, she was eager to chat a bit, but unfortunately she mostly wondered if I'd been able to find gainful employment.

"Have you found work yet?" she'd ask me, a slightly piteous look on her face.

"*Ancora no,*" was my usual response. For some reason her daily question, which may have only been for a lack of anything else to say, succeeded in putting pressure on me that I hadn't been putting on myself.

One day as I approached the *legatoria*, Gabriella leaned against the building smoking her mid-morning cigarette, speaking agitatedly to someone on her cell phone. Her long black hair swung to and fro as she paced, and she revealed a number of tattoos in her midriff-baring shirt—of the sort I hadn't been able to wear since I was a toddler. She waved quickly as I approached and finished her call.

"*Gli uomini?*" I asked as she followed me into the shop. Men?

"They love too much," she said cryptically. "Have you found work yet?"

"Not yet. But I went to that restaurant you suggested. They didn't seem to need anyone."

"I think it may be your Italian," she said as she began preparing the binding of a leather journal.

Gabriella didn't sugarcoat it. She was probably right since any kind of service job would require my dealing with customers in Italian. Of course, Gabriella spoke to me in English and thus continued to enable me. I'll admit it was difficult. I had a couple of rehearsed lines for job-hunting, but once the *proprietario* launched into any sort of explanation, I began treading in a sea of confusion and resorted to my intelligent nod, coupled with a "*Sì.*" Apparently this wasn't the best approach. Gabriella offered a gentle nudge in the direction of Italian lessons before telling me there was another alternative if I didn't find a job.

"You could always do what some girls do here: Marry a man with money." I studied Gabriella's face to see if she was joking. She wasn't. As she brushed glue into the binding of the journal, she explained, "We have lots of older men here, and if you marry an old one who is rich, you will have the money when he dies."

"I'll give it some thought," I told her. There were a lot of older men here indeed. Many more than I remembered from my last two trips. Of course, it had been colder on my visits, and they'd probably been tucked away under lap rugs in front of their fireplaces. My usual route from my house into town involved a steep winding shortcut, and along the way was a social club for retirees called Auser. Everyday, it was like running the gauntlet as I passed the cluster of white-haired men sitting in green plastic lawn chairs having their afternoon chat. I'd smile nervously as the conversation stopped. Some offered polite greetings, while others settled for not-so-polite leers at my chest. Perhaps my future husband was awaiting me there? Admittedly, I'd always had a thing for older men, but usually the ones I was attracted to weren't yet collecting their *pensioni.*

Gabriella continued to educate me on the social scene in Montepulciano as she worked. "There are many couples living together who not get married," she told me. I raised a brow, surprised at this disclosure. I'd assumed that most people were practicing Catholics and, like my friend Laura and her new husband Gianni, waited until after marriage to live together. Religion seemed such a part of the culture. I had just missed the yearly *benedizione* of the houses for which the parish priest went door to door and said a blessing for each home. I had no idea if our apartment had been blessed, but Marinella assured me that the blessing passed through seven walls, so I figured I was covered. But despite house blessings and several religious processions throughout the year, it seemed to me, at least from my new acquaintances, that practicing Catholics were in the minority; in fact, most Italians I knew were atheists, and one was even a Buddhist.

Gabriella pressed the journal shut, applying pressure to the cover to set the tacky glue before picking up the next one. She looked at me intently. "But remember," she finished wisely, "if you not get married, you not get the money."

❖   ❖   ❖

Attempting the tricky business of deflowering artichokes so I could toss them with my spaghetti later that day, I tugged and pulled at the outer leaves. The purple and green globes were so plentiful at the market that I'd been eating them in every way I could think of: steamed, stuffed, and today's project:

quartered, sautéed, and tossed with a bit of lemon and olive oil. Never quite knowing how many leaves to discard, I was elbow deep when Marinella called up to my window.

"Jennifer! *Oi! Che caldo, Madonnina!*"

"*Sì, caldo!*" I leaned from the sill.

"*Andiamo a fare una passeggiata ai Cappuccini?*"

I had no idea what that meant. It sounded like "Let's go for a cappuccino." Odd, since Italians don't drink their *cappuccini* in the afternoon, but I figured she just meant a coffee and was trying to say it in terms *l'americana* could understand. Marinella was quickly becoming a friend and confidant. We'd been spending time together over the last month sitting amiably together on the old wooden bench in the parking area, and I'd learned that Marinella could say more with a look than most people could say in five minutes of conversation. She was practical, strong, predictable (you could set your clock by her trips to the butcher), warm, suspicious. In short, a Tuscan mom.

And if you mentioned something she didn't like, she'd have you half-convinced that you were mistaken about the idea within a few minutes.

"But I love ricotta," I said to her one day while we were shopping together at the supermarket.

"*Noooo. A me non piace.*" The nose wrinkle that accompanied her simple statement was eloquent in its disapproval. I have since heard her "*non mi piace*" about everything from milk to Vino Nobile. "I drink *vino rosso*," she told me. "*E basta.*"

I was in awe of the way she could look at the clouds and predict rain. A region of farmers, Tuscany thrived on the coming of the rain, but who'd taught her? Her father had been a carpenter. How did she look at white, seemingly innocuous clouds and correctly predict "downpour in three hours?" And of course it always seemed to be on a day when I'd just hung out the laundry. "*Piove,*" she'd announce as she walked out her door with little more than a glance at the clouds. I'd gaze studiously at the sky trying to discern something other than the fluffy white pony of a cloud passing slowly overhead. When I asked her about it, she just pointed in a way that said, *Just look at it.* I nodded, saying "*Ho capito,*" while clearly having no idea. I now relied on Marinella's "*Piove*" announcements. When she brought in her laundry, I dragged mine in as well—she was almost never wrong.

So when I saw the way Marinella was dressed that afternoon upon meeting her downstairs, I realized I'd made an error. She was wearing shorts and athletic shoes. I had on jeans, a cute tank top, sandals, and my purse in hand. As we got in her car and she headed toward the countryside I now understood that we were going for a *walk.* Like exercise. I was excited at the prospect but desperately wished I could go back and change. And get my dog.

We drove through a country lane lined with elderly grand cypresses to an old monastery where I saw a sign for the fraternal order of . . . wait for it . . . Cappuccini. I chuckled, wishing my Italian was good enough to explain my mistake to Marinella. The Cappuccini, as I later learned, are Capuchin monks, and the brown color of their habits is said to have inspired the word *cappuccino,* for the similarly colored espresso-based drink.

The grounds of the monastery or *convento,* as they are called in Italy for both monks and nuns, were shaded by a forest of skinny birch trees. Within the high stone walls of the cloister, neatly trimmed rose bushes and stone planters brimming with gladiolas and crocuses softened the austerity, but paths along the outside of the wall had been left to nature; spring rain had resulted in riotous blooms of wildflowers peppering the lush grasses of the field. I caught the sweet scent of the yellow flowering vine I'd smelled on my walks with Cinder. *Ginestra,* Marinella gestured with a smile.

The path Marinella chose headed through the field and into the woods where it was shady, earthy-smelling and cool, and newly hatched mosquitoes swarmed us, dining as we walked. Rivulets had formed, and I accumulated a good amount of mud on my sandals from the boggy earth, even as I listened to Marinella talk about the attractive young couple Paolo and Carlotta, who were not in fact married, but *convivendo,* living together. I tried to discern if Marinella was disapproving, but she didn't seem to be. I'd chatted with Paolo when he was vacuuming his car, and his English had been good. Every time I'd said something in Italian, he'd replied in

English. The more I talked to him, the more I realized that Paolo was exactly the type of Italian man that fueled many a romantic fantasy. He worked in banking, liked to travel, was well-read, and spent time on his art in his garage whenever he got the chance. He was the walking definition of a Renaissance man.

Eventually, as it always does in Tuscany, the conversation turned to food. There are three essential herbs used in the Tuscan kitchen: parsley, rosemary, and sage. Marinella brought me samples of her ragù and *tagliatelle*, which she made by hand, and both were amazing. Almost every day she asked me "*Che cucini?*" What are you cooking? Food is such an essential part of this culture that she wasn't asking just to make conversation. She actually wanted to *know* what I was cooking. At first I didn't mind the question, but when it became pretty clear after a week or two that my lunches were not elaborate affairs of two courses (and most often were pasta tossed with cherry tomatoes, a salad, or a piece of fish), I found myself dreading having to come up with an answer. Unlike Marinella who had actual people to cook for, preparing pranzo for one was not particularly enjoyable.

Where were the recipes I thought I'd be learning?

Before I moved to Italy, I had visions of Italian women pulling me into their kitchens and imparting their centuries-old secrets, but as of yet, that hadn't come close to happening. So when I proudly told Marinella I had prepared her simple recipe with porcini mushrooms and even added some of the beautiful asparagus we'd found at the mercato, she wrinkled her nose. Apparently I was not allowed to tamper with the established *ricette* that have been prepared in the same manner for hundreds of years. This was Italia, where every woman seemed to spring forth from the womb with a ladle in one hand and innate sense of the tradition of cooking in the other.

"I'll teach you how to make my sauce and my ragù," Marinella declared as we headed back to the car. It was then I knew that Marinella had officially decided to take me under her wing—though I hoped she didn't have any expectation of me as a future daughter-in-law. Men living at home in their thirties were not a turn-on. Nonetheless, I told her I'd love to learn her recipes.

I may have been hopeless with the laundry, but maybe there was still hope for me with Tuscan cooking. And hey, at least next time I would be more appropriately dressed for the Cappuccini walk, so I was learning.

Piano, piano.

CHAPTER NINE

PARLA ITALIANO?

I l Sasso. I had walked by the little brass sign of the language school many times. Posted on a creamy-white stucco wall beside two skinny wooden doors, one of which was usually left ajar, it revealed nothing of what might lay beyond it. I had heard that the foreboding building had once been a medieval hospital complete with a foundling window for dropping off unwanted babies. The sign was well-polished, as if someone rubbed it each day for luck like the belly of a Buddha, and the words "*Scuola di Italiano per Stranieri*" etched in brass both attracted and repelled me. I knew I needed help. I just hated the idea of being thought of as a *straniera*. A foreigner.

"But I'm not a *straniera*," I'd argue to the sign each time I passed by. "I'm just ... new."

"Oh, but you are," the sign would reply in a patient, deep voice that suggested it was used to dealing with headstrong Americans trying to do things the hard way. In fact, the sign sounded just like my literature professor in college, Dr. Smart, who asked spectacularly difficult questions (which never seemed to have a real answer) and who'd always encourage us to see the other side of the argument. I half-expected the sign's next words to be, "Not that there's anything wrong with that."

But to the town of Montepulciano, I was and would always be a *straniera*. Luciana had introduced me as such to the attorney we'd met with, and I'd overhead Marinella saying it as well. I knew it was merely descriptive and not an insult, but it burned like one. And it's not just reserved for non-Italians; Italians identify each other as *milanese, napoletano,* or *sardo*—even if the person has lived in his adopted Italian location for thirty years, raised kids, paid taxes, and owned a shop.

Yes, I knew I'd forever be *L'americana.*

But then one day, something made me do it; I have a strong suspicion it had something to do with a desire to stop conversing with inanimate objects. So finally, I pushed open the door and stepped into the dark, cavernous hallway. Excitement and apprehension mingled in my stomach as though it were the first day of school, which I guess it was. Wandering the vast, echoing hall I wondered if I had strolled onto a replica of Hogwarts. This place must be filled with dark hallways and secret passageways, I thought, my imagination flooding with scenes and possibilities that had nothing to do with the Italian language.

The entry hall was lined with bookcases and low sofas for lounging, and the reassuring smell of books and stale pizza propelled me into the reception area where a blonde woman was playing the part of harried-but-capable receptionist. Speaking impatiently in rapid Italian, she held the phone to one ear while typing something on her computer and giving commiserating looks to the chubby young man waiting to speak with her. Her clipped Italian screamed "non-native" even to me.

Her name was Heike, and she was at once warm and brisk, interested but efficient. I learned in the half-hour I spent with her that she was German and had moved to Montepulciano because she'd married an Italian. I sensed that her capable ingenuity was somewhat stifled by the pace of the town. Her entire being radiated with "I can do so much more than I'm allowed to" energy and reminded me of a little kid bursting with anticipation, ready to shout "Watch me do this!"

The chubby American student, who'd been pacing around in flip flops and calf-length shorts, had apparently received some bad news in Italian from someone on the other end of his cell phone. He held the phone at arm's length, entreating Heike to take it. "I don't know what she's saying," he whined, clearly on the verge of tears. Heike took the phone, sussed out the problem in ten seconds, speaking in rapid Italian, then hung up and switched into English.

"Your credit card didn't go through. Get over to your hotel and give them another one." She whipped out a tissue and handed it and the cell phone back to the bewildered youth.

Visibly relieved, he thanked Heike and stumbled away. I attempted my opening in Italian, if only to show that I was indeed serious about becoming fluent, but after a few seconds of not understanding the questions flying at me in rapid succession, I switched to English.

Heike pulled me into an office, and we sat in chairs opposite each other. She tucked her serviceable blue sack dress around her legs as she perched on the edge of her chair, even as she kept one ear cocked for the phone. I had the impression I'd better not mince words.

"I need to be fluent in Italian," I told her. "I just moved here a month ago, and I can still barely speak. I need to be able to communicate so I can find a job. How long will it take?"

"You'll never be fluent," she told me with a shake of her blonde bob. "So give up that dream right now. I've been here twelve years, and I'm still not fluent. But after a few months your comprehension will improve enormously and it *will* make a difference."

Sold.

We settled on private lessons with a tutor five days a week for the first week and then a reevaluation. She handed me over to a professor, Silvia, who gave me a take-home test. "This will assess your skill set," she told me and then began asking me questions I couldn't really understand completely. I was trying so hard to respond correctly that I sounded awful, and I'm sure she stamped "Needs remedial assistance" on my file as I walked out of the room.

I spent the rest of the afternoon job-hunting, hoping my enthusiastic admission that I'd just signed up at Il Sasso for classes might curry some favor with potential employers. Heike had told me that the owner of Il Sasso also owned a restaurant, so I went there first. Head held high, I strolled into the bright, open, family-style restaurant with a large wood-burning pizza oven. Perfect. However, after I gave my rehearsed spiel to the manager, he didn't seem convinced that I could handle a waitress job. I'd worked as a waitress through high school, college, and part of law school, so I took some offense at his tone. Unfortunately, though, signing up for language classes didn't automatically give me a better vocabulary and ability to expound on my work history in Italian. He grudgingly scribbled my name and number on a waitlist that had four names ahead of mine, but I knew he'd never call.

After speaking with more and more shop owners and restaurant managers, I discovered that the problem wasn't my language skills so much as that the tourist season was just off that year. I chatted with the *proprietario* of a restaurant famous for its *bistecca fiorentina* longer than the others. He was balding and stern but told me he liked to hire Americans. This was the most encouraging thing I'd heard so far. I left feeling like this could be a possibility, but as I was walking out the door, I distinctly heard card stock being torn in half. My card stock. Had he really just ripped up my card before I even left the restaurant? My spirits deflated like a popped balloon; I couldn't bring myself to look back.

I could only hope that language school would at least give me the words to respond in such situations, but I knew it would be a while yet before that happened.

Pazienza.

CHAPTER TEN

FINDING MY QUINTY

I arrived bright and early for my first class at Il Sasso, take-home test in hand (attempted, if not fully completed), but my tutor, Valentina, never showed. I sat in a classroom for over a half-hour, at first making allowances for "Italian time," but then decided to leave because (a) I was spending money I couldn't really afford in order to take these lessons, and (b) even my law school professors hadn't required us to wait past a half-hour if they were running late.

Now, after numerous calls from Heike and Silvia apologizing up and down, I'd returned again. I'd barely reached Heike's desk when an older man strode in from an office, shorter than me with cropped, bristly gray hair and a matching bristly gray beard. I smiled as I watched him chat with Heike. He seemed affable and warm and had an endearing habit of continually checking his old-fashioned pocket watch, making me think of the white rabbit from *Alice in Wonderland*. *I'm late! I'm late for a very important date!*

Alberto escorted me down the hall to a small classroom overlooking a courtyard where I settled into a seat to wait for Valentina, pulling out my new leather journal and my now well-worn test. But a couple of minutes later Alberto came in, closing the door. "I'm going to do your lessons if that's OK with you," he told me. I arched a brow, dying to ask what had happened to Valentina but instead nodded. Was I so bad they'd brought out the big guns for me? Did Alberto, the owner of the school, enjoy the challenge of remedial students? Or was he some kind of masochist who couldn't wait to be tortured by my horrible pronunciation?

He studied my test for a couple of minutes and then, to my mortification, wanted to go over it together . . . out loud. No formal training in Italian, a reliance on my *OGGI IN ITALIA* textbook, slapdash lessons with my friend Alessandro, and my own woefully bad study habits combined to form gaps in my grammatical knowledge that made the Grand Canyon look like a gully.

But by the end of the two-hour lesson (during which time I'd spoken almost entirely in Italian), I'd gained a modicum of confidence. Unfortunately, I was also developing a crush on Alberto. It could have been the way he said "*Brava!*" every time I got even the simplest conjugation correct, or the way his intense amber eyes stared into mine as we talked. Or the way we shared intimate stories about our childhoods and families. Or the way his gaze skimmed my breasts whenever he thought I wasn't looking. Whatever it was, I knew I needed to nip it in the bud.

I listed his unattractive features on the way home, desperately talking myself out of a crush. Red pants. Not classically handsome. Too short. Too old. Oh yeah, lived with girlfriend. That was a biggie.

I mean, come on. First Alessandro. Now Alberto? What was it with me and Italian professors? I resolved to focus my energies on being a *brava studentessa* and to adopt "I will not flirt with my Italian professor" as my daily mantra, but then something caught my eye. I'd been skimming through a promotional booklet about the school when I saw Alberto's last name. I dropped everything and dug out my cell phone.

"I found my Quinty!" I shouted, jumping up and down as I laughed into the receiver.

The response on the other end, however, was not so enthusiastic. "You know I'm six hours behind right?" Will replied.

"Erm, yeah." I did a quick calculation and realized it was only five a.m. in New York.

"I'm thrilled you found Quinty. Call me when it's morning." Click.

✦   ✦   ✦

Will had come on my last trip to Italy, and thus began the legend of Quinty. Before our trip we'd watched the film *My House in Umbria* three or four times. In the story, a woman named Mrs. Delahunty invites survivors of a terrorist attack on a train to convalesce at her Umbrian estate. She is an aging writer who drinks a little too much, speaks and writes in flowery language, and tries to project an image of a carefree novelist; her faithful companion is Quinty. Sure, he prepares her cocktails and drives her around, but more than that, he looks out for her.

Will and I *loved* the movie. So much so that on our trip to Italy we delighted in speaking in Mrs. Delahunty's flowery language, and he insisted that after my move it was inevitable that I'd become her, i.e., flirting inappropriately, exposing my décolletage, and attempting to play the role of carefree novelist. Will, for his part, would have to relinquish the role of Quinty, which he performed admirably on our trip, driving me all around Tuscany and Umbria, keeping the wine flowing and being a good friend even after spending long periods of time in close quarters with me.

So this is why I neglected to check time zone differences when I realized my Italian professor's name was none other than Alberto Quinty. (OK, it was spelled Quinti, but close enough!)

After waiting for a decent hour of the morning, I sent Will the photo I'd snapped in class that morning, relaying the story. Will, having survived many of my crushes in the past, made his usual snarky commentary on my attraction to older men, as well as my propensity for getting myself into many Lucy Ricardo-like scrapes.

"What happened to the fruit guy?" he asked. "I thought he was your latest crush."

I brushed aside all mention of Salvatore. It was true we'd been bantering back and forth, but he'd left for the summer to cultivate his orchards in Sicily. Surely I was allowed more than one flirtation. It was Italy, after all.

I endured the "*Luuucy!*" groan from Will, who felt the need to remind me that I was living in a small town. "You have the rest of your life to flirt with Italians. Don't get into trouble in your first month."

Now what would be the fun of that? I thought, already trying to figure out what sexy tops I had in my wardrobe for my next lesson.

L'avventura, right?

CHAPTER ELEVEN

THE GOOD, THE BAD, AND THE...DIO MIO

I sat in Alberto's minivan in the parking area behind his restaurant. Before he could start the engine, I pulled a wrapped present from my bag and handed it to him. He stared at me quizzically, so I explained it was a birthday gift.

"*Bello!*" he said as he opened the Elizabeth George novel I'd bought for him. His face registered the same happiness I feel upon encountering a new book. He'd mentioned in class that his birthday was the following day, and I knew from our talks that he liked her work, so I thought I would get him a little something. The gift would also work as a thank you for his offer to run me out to Laura's farm to pick up the rest of my boxes. It was the end of May, and I'd been living without my belongings for over a month. I didn't want to keep bugging Laura and Marisa, but I needed my clothes. I'd resorted to buying a few things at the Conad, the town supermarket, but it wasn't the same as having my own stuff.

Alberto basically knew my whole life story now. So, after hearing me mention my lack of clothing and household belongings in class and my decision to just get a taxi out there, he'd offered to take me.

After twenty hours of class together, we'd exhausted a lot of topics, but mainly he asked me questions about my daily routine and the things I was learning about Montepulciano, laughing at my observations on the differences between Montepulciano and New York: how the "street sweeper" here was a little old man with a homemade twig broom; the fact that most people didn't seem to receive mail every day, and that one young blonde woman delivered the mail for the whole town; how I was pretty sure that the man who picked up my garbage was also a bus driver and that I sometimes felt as if I were in a movie in which one character was playing multiple roles. We'd talked about everything from my outings to the market and what I was buying and cooking to whom I was meeting and what I did in the evenings. He basically just tried to keep me talking in Italian.

As for him, I knew he hated oregano, loved chocolate, oversalted his food, wished he had more free time, shared my fear of driving on steep cliff roads, and that he was a rapacious reader.

I'd expressed my worries over finding a job, my favorite brioche at the bar (chocolate cream-filled), and my initial confusion with the system of garbage. I mean, what was with the elaborate colored bag scheme for each type of refuse, including plastic, paper, regular garbage, and garden trimmings? I, of course, had none of these bags since Luciana hadn't provided them, nor did I know which days were for what. Instead, I found out the hard way when I was lectured in rapid Italian by my annoyed garbage collector/bus driver on the proper days for pickup of each—a conversation in which I understood the tone but not the content.

Another valuable bit of garbage knowledge was that there was no pickup on Sunday. This didn't pose a problem unless you decided to, say, have fish on Saturday because then you had to live with your stinky fish garbage in the house until Monday morning. You weren't allowed to leave it on the street at night, and even if you took that liberty, the stray cats would mangle it to pieces.

In our rambling conversations about nothing and everything, though, we also found moments of levity and were able to connect on a silly level as well— and one particular exchange about another skirmish with my Italian nemesis, the laundry, actually led to Alberto's offer to take me to retrieve my things at the agriturismo.

That morning I was slightly behind schedule because I'd been finishing up my homework. After I completed my assignment, I hung my laundry outside, and then took Cinder out for a quick walk. I caught the scent of the jasmine along Marinella's fence and inhaled deeply. That's when I glanced up at the laundry line onto which I'd just wrangled my sopping wet, enormous duvet cover. But instead of seeing my laundry, I saw nothing. The duvet cover and laundry cord lay in a heap in the gravel.

"*Vaffanculo!!!*"

The Italian curse hurtled out of me, resoundingly loud in the morning quiet as I stomped over to retrieve my laundry. Then I studied the fractured cord and the window above. What feats of gymnastics would I have to attempt to install a new one? And more importantly, how could I do it without returning to that same woman at the hardware store?

I fumed all the way to class, for which I was now late.

"*Tutto a posto?*" Alberto had asked when he saw my face.

I regaled him with a dramatic recitation of my laundry woes, then I saw him trying to stifle a smile.

"*Una piccola cosa,*" he told me. A small thing. Sure, easy for him to say; he probably had a dryer. "At least you're in Tuscany, right?" he added with a mischievous smile.

I had told him far too much about my life, apparently, including my motto, but I choked out a laugh and felt myself beginning to smile in return. As we went on with class I was in slightly better humor, although I still wasn't sure how I was going to repair the laundry cord. When Alberto asked me what I was doing for the weekend, I mentioned my plan to take a taxi to pick up my boxes. Perhaps feeling badly that I had no one to help me with yet another "*piccola cosa,*" Alberto volunteered his van for the project.

We arrived at the agriturismo to find Laura and Marisa busy cleaning the guest rooms. They came out to say hello, leaning over the balcony of the apartment that I thought of as mine since I'd stayed in it on two of my visits. I felt a little disappointed that they didn't even come down to greet me. I introduced Alberto as he helped me load the boxes into the back of his van.

They spouted off in rapid Italian while I stood there picking up every tenth word. "*Non ho capito niente,*" I offered finally, and then jokingly added that

Alberto must be a terrible teacher since I still couldn't understand anything after twenty hours of class.

"*Lei è una pigra studentessa,*" he shot back with a smile, directing his gaze at me. I wanted to protest, but it was true; I *was* a lazy student. Laura and Marisa laughed, shaking their heads at my terrible misfortune.

We could only chat for another minute before it was time to go. I felt oddly bereft as we got ready to drive away: I didn't want to leave. I wanted to be there on the farm helping them. *This* was the life I'd envisioned for myself. These were the friends I was supposed to be spending time with.

"I miss you guys," I said in parting, but it felt inadequate.

"*Ci vediamo,*" Laura said.

I didn't believe her.

CHAPTER TWELVE

I NUOVI AMICI

Perhaps I'd won them over with my repeated visits, or perhaps they simply realized I wasn't going away, but over the next few weeks, the neighborhood folk started coming around, and I finally began making friends.

First it was Caterina and Gabriella. We'd graduated from two-minute chats in their stores to actual conversations about our days, our friends, our families.

"*Ciao*, Jenny," Gabriella would call while mopping the floor of her shop as I hiked up the hill to class at Il Sasso.

"*Dove vai?*" Caterina smiled as she artfully arranged her baskets laden with homemade pastas and dried herbs in front of the cheese shop.

"*Vado a scuola,*" I'd tell them, making a silly face and a comment about my homework to make them laugh. After class, I'd stop in to recount my lesson and buy a little something. Or, if they were outside having a smoke, we could chat at length without the constant interruption of their customers.

There was also Antonella at her *alimentari*, or grocery store. Mid-forties, curvy, and blonde, she had a husky laugh that drove the men wild. Young, old, all the men loved her, and never mind that she had a husband and three kids, she flirted right back and was quick with the banter and playful comments. I liked her right away. I'd stop in to buy eggs or pancetta and end up buying lots of other things I didn't need while chatting with her. Antonella never rushed me when I tried to form sentences, and if someone came in and we weren't done talking she'd say "*In fretta?*", asking me if I was in a hurry.

"No, of course not," I'd say, and we'd continue our chat after her customer left. We both had a passion for chocolate, and I'd made my PMS brownies for her and the other girls the week before. I had a tough time translating "PMS," but the ladies trusted me when I assured them that these brownies cured that and a host of other ailments.

The day was brilliantly sunny and hot as I swung open the narrow wooden door of Il Sasso that morning, looking forward to my lesson. I was determined to master prepositions or die trying.

"I called the *comune* to find out what paperwork you need so that you can work," Alberto told me before I'd even pulled out my homework. Hooray! Was he going to find a place for me in his restaurant? Then he added, "You'd better sit down."

As it turned out, while my residency was *tutto a posto*, this didn't mean I could work. It meant *after* my citizenship application was complete I could work. This could be months away because I was still waiting for that damn document from the US. Not good news.

"Can you survive the year without working?" Alberto asked as I sat, stunned, trying to process this information. Was he kidding? Perhaps the fact that I was a struggling writer got lost in translation somewhere?

"Honestly, I can probably survive until November or December. If I don't eat, and Cinder doesn't eat, maybe January. Maybe."

That's when Alberto and I discussed working "*in nero.*" This is basically working "under the table." Cash. Off the books. I'd forgotten about this. Surely there must be employers who hired this way, right? *Ristoranti? Agriturismi?* The look on Alberto's face let me know that I was screwed.

Tears hovered as he explained that here in Italy, everything was rigorously controlled and checked. Sure, it was done, but it was risky for an employer (meaning him) to hire someone *in nero*, because if someone asked questions, there was a tremendous fine.

"Can't I just slip out the back?" I joked. My stomach roiled. What would I do if I couldn't work? Alberto took my hand to comfort me, and for a minute I felt a little better.

"Teaching English lessons and jobs of that nature you can do without too much concern," he told me. My mind flashed to that English lessons flyer I had never put up. "And as soon as your paperwork is complete, you'll find something I'm sure. *Coraggio.*"

Telling me to keep my strength up didn't help much as I envisioned all of my business cards sitting at restaurants and stores all over town. Now if someone actually needed an employee, I would have to explain my situation and pray someone took the risk. I thanked Alberto for his help, packed up my things, and left.

Visibly upset, I wandered into Antonella's shop and began scanning her shelves for chocolate as if it were a biological imperative. Spying an enormous jar of Nutella, I had to call upon my deepest reserves of self-control to keep from launching myself at it. Seeing my wild-eyed look, Antonella quickly snatched a chocolate cookie from the display case and thrust it at me.

"*Che cosa è successo?*"

As I began telling her, she grabbed my arm and led me outside where Caterina and Gabriella were sitting on a stoop having a cigarette. Obviously this news called for a conference. The girls were often here together and although I typically stopped to chat for a few minutes, I never lingered too long because I still felt a little awkward. But today Caterina scooted over and, for the first time, motioned for me to sit down and join them.

I explained again what was going on, and Caterina told me not to worry. She said lots of restaurants hired *in nero* and began reeling them off.

"Start with Andre at La Caverna," she told me. "He can be rude, but he's fair." Then the three of them encouraged me to get my flyers ready, saying they'd post them and start spreading the word about English lessons. In less than ten minutes, I was feeling much better—slightly nauseated again, this time from the smoke and the cookie, but better. I could make this work.

I was supposed to be here, and I could make this work.

I had to.

I grabbed the Nutella just in case.

✦   ✦   ✦

After a quick change and a regrouping, I headed over to La Caverna to speak with Andre. Stepping into the restaurant, tucked away on a side street, was indeed like descending into an underground cavern. Constructed in a series of subterranean grottos that held grain in time immemorial, the cave boasted low, curved ceilings, giving the restaurant a romantically lit, cool, and elegantly appointed atmosphere.

From his name, or maybe because Caterina had said he was rude, I'd assumed Andre was French but the tall handsome man who greeted me was all smiles, flirtatious, and most definitely Italian. I told him that Caterina had given me his name and that I was looking for work. We chatted for a few minutes, and he showed more than a polite amount of interest in the idea of my working for him. I flirted back a little since at this point I just needed a job.

But as I was gathering my nerve to explain about working *in nero*, a stern-looking woman emerged from the kitchen. Andre introduced her as his wife. I'd never fully appreciated the expression "a black look" before meeting Alba. The perma-scowl on her face told me quite clearly she did not appreciate my lighthearted banter with her husband—and that this behavior wasn't anything novel for him.

Andre, not losing a beat, finished the introductions and said he'd like to find a place for me in the restaurant. "My English is excellent," I said jokingly to Alba, desperate to erase that look on her face.

"Do you have your *permesso* to work?" she asked. Crap. I didn't have a work permit, so I launched into an explanation of my citizenship application and how I had to wait before I could work "officially." I looked to Andre, hoping for some sort of "wink wink," but he averted his eyes. Obviously, if he did hire people *in nero*, he wasn't about to broadcast it.

"*Che schifo.*" Alba spat the words at me. "*Questo è un grosso problema in Italia.*" She then carried on a two-minute diatribe about working *in nero* and how it was destroying Italy. "*Schifo, schifo,*" she repeated, employing more venom with each utterance. Was she calling me disgusting, or my situation? I didn't want to know the answer.

When she was finished, she turned on her heel and stalked back to the kitchen like a lioness returning to her den.

The *discussione* was *finita*.

Andre tried to be jovial after she left, but it was quite obvious who made the decisions. I left my card anyway, thanking him for his time. Tears stung my eyes as I headed home, but I refused to give way to them. Who wanted to work in a dark old cave anyway?

CHAPTER THIRTEEN

CHE CUCINI?

I f there is anything sexier than a man who cooks, it has to be a man who is a professional chef and who teaches cooking classes. Specifically, a beautiful chef named Fabio who teaches cooking classes in Montepulciano. I'm not kidding, that's his name.

"I need a favor," Alberto told me in class one morning. My mind raced at the possibilities. Someone to accompany him on a long walk in the countryside? A date for the theater? Remember the female student from *Raiders of the Lost Ark* who put the "Love You" on her eyelids so that only Professor Jones could see it when she blinked? I was a tad worried I was slowly becoming that girl. Alberto must have seen that he'd lost me because he began again.

"Can I ask you a favor? There is an Australian writer who wants to enroll in a baking class. She can't speak Italian yet, and the chef doesn't speak English. If you'd be willing to translate for the class, you can have the lesson for free, and I'll give you an extra lesson with me gratis as well."

I think I may have shouted my "*Sì*," because Alberto looked a little startled. What was there to think about?

Cooking class. LOVE.

Extra class with Alberto. LOVE.

It would only have been better if he'd offered to pay me instead of giving me an extra class, but he intimated that if it worked out maybe he could the next time, and that further upped my hopes that my big break was just around the corner. The only really befuddling part of the proposition was why, after only a few weeks, I was the go-to person at the school for translation. I guessed I should have been pleased Alberto thought my Italian was improving to the point that I could adequately do the job, but the prospect of anyone relying on me to learn how to make a proper *tiramisù* was terrifying.

When the day of the cooking lesson arrived, I was prepared. I had reviewed cooking terms, Googled the author, Kate, checked out her website, and even read some reviews of her books.

At three thirty sharp, I was at the town's gate, and Kate arrived right after me; her friend Sally trailed behind.

They were an odd pair. Kate was tall and painfully thin with sharp angles jutting out all over; it was hard to believe she ate food let alone wanted to cook it. Sally was petite, soft, and curvy. They'd met at Il Sasso and were taking language classes together. Neither of them seemed to have absorbed much Italian in the week they'd been here, though. Lucky for me!

It wasn't a long walk to the agriturismo for the cooking classes, but I'd never been there before. Kate had forgotten the map that Heike had given her, and all I could remember from Alberto's directions were "tennis courts." I had visions of the three of us wandering hopelessly around the Tuscan countryside for hours, but as we strolled down the mountain and passed the bus station, I spotted the tennis courts off to the left. I began to relax and take in the rural and gorgeous land opening up before us. An expanse of vineyards stretched out alongside the road.

Did we just step into a movie set or what?

As I talked with the women, answering their questions about being an expat in Montepulciano, it felt strange to be having a full conversation in English. I found myself replying in Italian more than once. Kate was in Italy researching a novel about a woman who moves to Montepulciano and learns to bake, and Sally was an artist traveling around Italy seeking inspiration. Next stop? Venice.

"I can't get used to this," Sally said as another impossibly picturesque vista greeted us over the next rise. "It's too beautiful. Do you pinch yourself everyday that you're actually living here?"

"I do. The view from my apartment is unreal. I keep wondering if the people who live here really understand how magnificent this place is or if to them it's like a beautiful piece of art hanging in the living room—stunning but you're so used to it that you don't even glance at it when you enter the room."

Kate, impatient with our "beautiful countryside" chatter, turned the conversation back to her and her book. "So I'm hoping this chef is competent." Her voice was a tad shrill and out of place among the peace of the countryside. "I'm a very good baker myself; my cakes have won prizes in Australia, but I really need to learn how to make the desserts of Tuscany. For the book."

Sally and I exchanged looks. Hers communicated, *She's nice once you get to know her, really,* while mine said, *Conceited much?* Not once during our twenty-minute walk did Kate inquire as to what type of writing I did, which in my experience is odd, particularly for a fellow writer.

So I was happy when we finally sighted the sprawling stone farmhouse of the agriturismo. Beautifully restored and nestled among acres of grapevines, the old building effectively disguised its entrance; we wandered around trying to find a door until we bumped into Fabio. Alberto had neglected to mention that he was *bello. Bellissimo* even. Brown hair, emerald eyes, and a smile that in a pinch could surely melt butter. He was buttoned up in a black chef's shirt, and initial introductions were formal. We followed him from the stone terrace through a large dining room with wood-beamed ceilings and tables set with starched linen tablecloths, and as he bent over to reach inside a cabinet in search of aprons for us, I glanced at Sally and smothered a giggle. I could see her thoughts were on the same track as mine: The men here were just too pretty.

Fabio showed us around the kitchen, which was modern and shiny with stainless steel. A young woman worked in a corner cutting and rolling *pici* for the agriturismo's hungry guests. A ragù simmered on the stove.

As we fastened our aprons, Fabio explained the desserts we would be making: *cantucci, torta della nonna,* blackberry *crostata,* and a *tiramisù.* Suddenly I remembered my purpose and undertook to explain each of them in English, which was slow-going.

Fabio began pulling out eggs, flour, and butter for us to work with.

"Who wants to go first?" he asked. I looked to Kate since this was her class, but she picked up her notebook.

"Go ahead," she told me. "I'll take notes."

"*Ci provo*," I said to Fabio, then washed my hands, watching as he put a hunk of butter on a wooden board. He told me to soften it, making smushing motions with his hands. My usual method of softening butter involved letting it come to room temperature and sometimes putting it near my preheating oven, but I was game to smush some butter, cool and slippery as it slid between my fingers. I let go of my self-consciousness and soon felt an almost child-like enthusiasm for creating something with my hands. When Fabio was satisfied that it was ready, he added sugar to my board, and I began kneading that into the butter. Next came the flour and egg. We were making *pasta frolla*, the pastry crust used for tarts and the famous *torta della nonna*, or grandma's cake. I wanted to remember the amounts, but I was too preoccupied trying to keep my wayward eggs from escaping the well of my flour wall while translating Kate's many questions for Fabio.

"Why are the eggs so orange?" she asked. The yolks of Italian eggs are often a rich orangey yellow, like the color of the sun as it begins its descent in the evening. I was sure it had something to do with the food Italian chickens ate, so I told her this since Fabio either thought the question was ridiculous or beneath him and simply didn't answer.

My egg knowledge did extend to another little tidbit I had learned in my time in Italy: Italians didn't refrigerate their eggs. I was still slightly suspicious of this practice, especially since I'd once had to chuck a batter of brownies because one of the eggs was rotten and emanated a stink like you can't imagine when I cracked it open. Since then, I've cracked each egg individually before adding it to the batter just to be safe.

Fabio stood silent, arms crossed as he waited for me to finish with the dough. My hands were sticky and covered in floury goo, but in one fluid movement Fabio took over, pulled the excess flour mixture off of my hands in a strangely erotic way, incorporated the dough fully, and formed it into a disc. When he finished, his hands weren't even gunky. I looked at Sally.

How sexy was that?

Kate jumped in for the second recipe, *tiramisù*, and by then I'd gotten the hang of the translating, doing my best to interject some comedy into my give-and-take with Fabio. I wondered if he was married.

"Jenny? *Mi hai sentito?*" Fabio asked. He, Kate, and Sally were all staring at me expectantly. Oops. I had to rescue my mind from non-culinary territory.

"Erm, sorry, ladies," I quipped. "Our chef is just too handsome. I lost my concentration."

Hearing laughter behind me, I spun around. Fabio winked at me. I then realized that while Fabio didn't "speak" English, he understood it well enough. My face flamed redder than the bubbling tomato sauce on the stove.

While Kate whipped the mascarpone for her *tiramisù*, I took notes for her, jotting down ingredients, cooking times, and instructions while Sally snapped photos. We began the custard for the *torta della nonna*, then the blackberry tart. With each dessert, Kate repeated that she wanted to do the cooking herself. Fabio looked askance at me, and I shrugged and rolled my eyes. I was beginning to feel like we were the servants of some celebrity chef. But ours was domineering and had awful technique.

"No problem," I told Kate, forcing cheerfulness. "It's your class." And you look ridiculous in that paper hat.

While Kate took a break to use the bathroom, I asked Sally what the deal was.

"She told me I could come, but I couldn't participate," Sally said in the tone of the long-suffering sidekick. "I thought she was joking, but then she said it again while we were walking to meet you."

"That's ridiculous," I told her. "What's the fun of a cooking class if you don't get to cook?"

Sally shrugged helplessly. She'd come thinking this class was going to be a fun afternoon of Tuscan baking and instead had to stand around on the sidelines. I briefly contemplated screwing up the recipes so Kate couldn't recreate them, but then remembered that Fabio was supposed to send her copies too, so she'd be able to spot any inconsistencies. Plus, I didn't want to make a *brutta figura*, bad impression, with Alberto and risk other translation work.

Our last dessert was the *cantucci*, which are small biscotti-like cookies that this area is famous for—crunchy, perfect for dipping in your coffee or Vin Santo or for spreading a little Nutella on, as Gabriella liked to do. They are typically made with either almonds or hazelnuts, and Fabio's recipe called for hazelnuts. Kate formed the dough into logs, and Fabio transferred them to cookie sheets. Their sweet scent filled the room as they baked, and when they came out of the oven, Fabio asked me to slice the rolls into small cookies. Kate looked as if she might protest, but Fabio ignored her. He demonstrated how he wanted me to slice them at a slight angle, then covered my hands with his as I did the first couple. I closed my eyes for a moment, breathing in his smell of freshly baked cookies and tart, trying to be mindful of the sharp knife and my fingers.

Sally gave me a thumbs-up and snapped a picture. Kate, displeased that Fabio was letting me work, fumed and gulped down some of the agriturismo's wine that Fabio had just offered us. As we finished all of the desserts, Fabio plated them and presented them to us so that we could sample our work. The *torta della nonna* needed to cool for a few hours because the custard had been enveloped in the baking crust, so we wouldn't get to try that. Fabio, perhaps in an effort to assuage our disappointment, showed us an old scar earned from handling molten custard before it had cooled.

I crunched into the nuttiness of the *cantucci* and let the richness of the espresso and cream of the *tiramisù* dissolve in my mouth. I bit into the blackberry tart, the sweet tanginess of the blackberries exploding on my tongue. *Bliss.* The crust was buttery and light, and I felt some satisfaction that I'd prepared the dough, which we used for both the tart and the *torta della nonna*. Fabio didn't sample anything, nor was he drinking any wine. This was no doubt the reason he was in such optimal shape. It wasn't every day you saw a good cook or pastry chef without a *pancia*, stomach paunch. Sally and I sipped our wine and flirted freely with him. Kate asked some more questions for her book, which I then relayed to Fabio. We shared a conspiratorial "How annoying is she?" smile.

When it was time for us to leave, Fabio invited us to come back any time. "Be careful," I warned him with a wink, "I live nearby."

He raised an eyebrow, and my stomach did a little flip flop when he grinned at me. "I've moved here for good," I told him.

"Good. Then I'm sure we'll see each other." His hand lingered on mine a moment before I left with an irrepressible smile stretched from ear to ear.

Speriamo! Let's hope so!

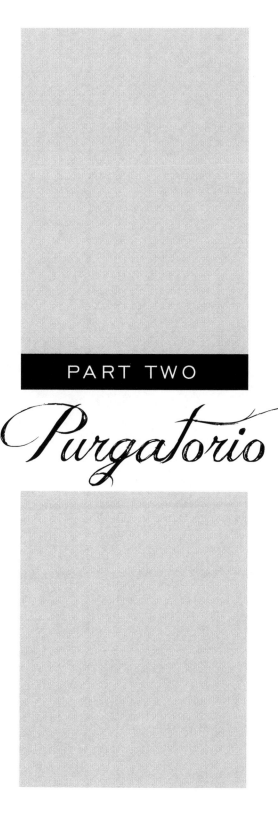

PART TWO

Purgatorio

CHAPTER FOURTEEN

BREAKDOWN ON THE CORSO

After the cooking class, I'd felt confident there would be other "jobs" with the school—Alberto had said as much in class—so I hadn't been freaking out so much about my rapidly dissipating nest egg. But as weeks went by and there were no further requests for my help, my anxiety grew. No jobs, and my repeated passes at restaurants and shops continued to yield nothing.

Niente.

Alberto took off on a two-week vacation for the Val D'Aosta, but before he left, perhaps sensing my preoccupation with work, he'd suggested I drop off my English lesson flyers around town, including at the agriturismo where I'd had my cooking class with Fabio. A capital idea, since the thought of seeing Fabio again certainly buoyed my spirits.

While Alberto was away, I stopped by Il Sasso one evening to see if I could get an email address or phone number for Fabio to set up an appointment. I ran into Silvia, the professor who'd given me my initial Italian take-home test. She sighed when she saw me, in a hurry to head home to her son, but obligingly rebooted her computer.

"He never responds," she warned as she scrolled her email contacts for his address. "I'm still waiting for the recipes from your class. That Australian writer is hounding me daily because I had told her I would forward them to her."

"I wouldn't feel too badly," I said with some glee. "I wrote out all of the recipes for the woman as if I were her secretary. They are in English and have notes and everything. But I'll ask Fabio about them when I see him."

"I'd appreciate that. And maybe I can send some students for English lessons your way." She left *if you get the recipes* unsaid.

I promised to get them, already mentally adding the payment from my future students to my bank account. How hard could it be to secure a few recipes?

◆　　◆　　◆

A few days passed and Fabio hadn't responded to my email, so I resolved to go in person and take my chances. The day was hot, unseasonably humid for June, so I put on a skirt, sandals, and a light tank top. I trekked along, perspiration forming between my breasts and just about everywhere else; the journey seeming really long this time, especially without anyone to talk to. When I spied the grapevines of the agriturismo, my spirits lifted briefly until I saw that the road was gated. Padlocked. What? In the middle of tourist season? I looked around to see if I could vault the fence or if I could attract someone's attention but then spotted a tiny handwritten sign tacked on a fence post. From the electric company. I couldn't understand all of it but gleaned that power had been shut off on the whole road for a week while work was being done. No Fabio. No recipes.

Argh. I dejectedly kicked a rock along the road on my way back, thunder in the distance echoing my frustration. Within five minutes black clouds had rolled in and the skies released their fury. Drenched, I picked up the pace, water squishing noisily out of my sandals. My sheer tank was plastered to my skin by the time I approached the walls of the town, and I broke into a sprint, no doubt revealing much more of my assets to Montepulciano that day than I would have liked.

On my second attempt, I decided to kill two birds with one stone (or as the Italians say "*prendere due piccioni con una fava*") and dragged Cinder along for a walk. The day was hot, but at least there was no sign of storm clouds. I couldn't handle another drenching. This time the gate was open, but I couldn't find anyone. It was still pranzo, but I'd tried to time it so that it was late pranzo, when everyone would be getting back to work. When my repeated knocks went unanswered, I resisted the urge to scream my frustration at the grapevines.

I was scribbling a note to Fabio when a door opened from an apartment above the restaurant. Fabio emerged . . . in a towel. *Soaking wet*! I'd obviously interrupted his shower. His entire body was tanned and glistening with tiny drops of water. If ever in my life I were going to swoon, please let it be now.

"The writer, right?" he said, shaking his head like a dog as he walked down the steps before offering his killer grin. "Who lives nearby."

I had no words. Instead, I mutely I pulled out my flyer and handed it to him. He read it. "I'd be happy to post it for you," he said.

"Um, thanks. I haven't found work yet." My mind went blank, and I couldn't form any other coherent sentences in Italian, my eyes glued to his naked chest.

"*Ciao*," I mumbled, then bolted, Cinder trailing in my wake. When I was safely out of his magnetic pull, which had sucked every rational thought out of my head, I remembered that I'd never asked him about the recipes.

Porca miseria!

Cinder gave me a disgusted look, telling me I was incompetent, would never find work, and that she was likely to starve.

"Don't worry," I told her as we trudged back up the mountain. "I'll send him an email about the recipes. And I'm sure it's just a matter of time before I find *something*."

❖   ❖   ❖

By July, I still had no recipes, and on the job front I was in full-on panic mode. My backup plan, which was vague but included begging Alberto for help, couldn't be put into effect yet. He'd returned from his vacation the week before, but despite two emails on my end, hadn't gotten in touch to schedule our next lesson.

If there was a silver lining—and as an optimist I was obligated to dig one from the ground with my bare and bleeding hands—it was that I was getting a little more proficient with my Italian. This was because I'd been spending time every evening hanging out with friends on the street.

In addition to Gabriella, Antonella, and Caterina, I'd gotten to know some of the male shop owners as well. There was the *macellaio*, or butcher, Silvano, whose shop was right across the street from Gabriella's and one door down from Caterina's. Antonella called him a busybody, and it was true that he did know everything about everyone. His shop opened early so he spent a fair amount of time on the street watching the comings and goings of his neighbors—if someone had just died, you could be sure to hear about it from Silvano before it was even posted on the town notice board. Built like he spent his days easily hefting sides of beef, he looked intimidating as he held court behind the glass display cases of meat. White hair shorn close, buzzed, and a faint scar that ran from his left eyebrow down his cheek added to the image. I wondered if he'd gotten the scar in a fight or if an irate customer hadn't been happy with his cuts of meat and exacted revenge. But then Silvano would smile, revealing a gap between his teeth, and he instantly became cute and boyish. He sliced and ground his clients orders, always jovial and eager for a joke, but his butcher's ensemble of white lab coat and cap had just enough blood sprinkled on them to make you remember he was the real deal. I hadn't bought much from Silvano mostly because I had no idea what to ask for when I went into the cool and immaculately clean shop. The red blobs of meat all looked the same to me, so if I did want to buy something, my pointing method didn't work well. Instead I had to describe what I was cooking and then Silvano reached into the case and pulled out a hunk of whatever he thought was appropriate for what I was describing. So far, this rather blundering approach had worked OK. I did learn when I decided to make hamburgers to mark the Fourth of July, that in Tuscany they call them *svizzere* or *svizzerine*, as apparently their introduction to Italy came from Switzerland.

The other two regulars who emerged from their shops when things were slow were Giuseppe and Niccolò. In his late-thirties and adorable, Niccolò had a cleft chin and sexy grin reminiscent of a young Dennis Quaid. Jeans were stacked in piles along the walls of his corner shop. "The first jean shop in Montepulciano," he proudly told me. "Started by my grandfather." Like Gabriella, Niccolò spoke some English so he would often translate for me some of the more difficult conversations—like when Silvano let everyone know *polmone* would be available the next morning.

"Lung," Niccolò said to me.

"I'll be sure to get here early," I joked. Were they really talking about lung with the same enthusiasm I use when talking about chocolate?

"It may sound strange, but it's delicious," he assured me. "First you must boil it, but then you cook it with a little oil, onions, carrots, celery, and tomato."

I nodded, smiling gamely. True, I wanted to increase my Tuscan repertoire of recipes, but *polmone* was going to be at the bottom of my list; even with lots of ingredients disguising it, it was still lung.

Giuseppe sold gnomes. And not just gnomes, but tiny gnome tree houses, fairies, bells, and other fanciful woodland creatures. His shop looked like a fantasyland and children happily stood three deep to take in the wonders. Mid-fifties with longish graying hair, wire glasses, and somewhat awkward, Giuseppe seemed perfectly suited to living among the creatures of this magical world. He rarely came out of his shop unless someone called to him. "*Arrivo*," he'd then respond, tentatively poking his head out like a turtle from his shell and approaching the group with a gnome or fairy clutched in his hand, as if counting on it to help make conversation.

There was something rather cozy about having a chat on a stoop with people I was getting to know. I'd felt more than a little relief that I was finally being accepted as part of the community.

"*Italiana in prova*," Antonella had dubbed me. An Italian in training!

In my first weeks, the reserve emanating from everyone felt as if I were butting up against an invisible wall. When I pictured myself living here, I'd assumed everyone would greet me enthusiastically. What I didn't realize was that these Tuscans were not the arms-thrown-open, come-stay-with-us-anytime Italians I'd encountered in some of my travels. It's not that they were cold, but there was a definite bubble around them that was difficult to penetrate. But once I was allowed inside, a light switched on after weeks of darkness. At first it was disorienting, but then I felt great relief and happiness.

Because there wasn't much activity in and out of the building with the stoop, it was a perfect place for everyone to congregate, smoke a cigarette, and still keep an eye on their stores. They all seemed to have an innate sense of which people were actually going to buy something and which would just browse for a minute and depart. The world walked by—tourists licking melting gelato or carrying precious bottles of newly purchased *vino* as well as residents going about their daily routine, older ladies prettily dressed for Mass and local misfits and personalities. I'd been watching this activity for over two months, but now my vantage point had changed as I was welcomed into the fold. I could now express my curiosity about people I'd seen. I prompted Antonella, "Tell me about that sharply dressed little old man with the pompadour," and I learned he was one of the richest men in town and tight with his money. His suits were immaculate but so old as to be considered vintage.

Conversations with my new friends ranged from intimate chats with one or two people at a time in which we learned about each other's history, to larger groupings in which everything was discussed from the weather to the lack of tourists this summer to local politics (which I couldn't follow at all yet), and, of course, lots of talk of recipes and food. Most afternoons I sat between Antonella and Caterina forming the third panel of the stoop's triptych. Slowly, the others would join in, Silvano always being the first, but Gabriella and Niccolò were never far behind.

The chats involving cultural differences were the most interesting to me.

"Why are Americans always portrayed as carrying enormous cups of coffee on television shows?" asked Niccolò, which led to a twenty-minute discussion of coffee, the amount both cultures work, quality of life, and the media.

Commentary on someone's nail polish sparked off a heated debate about beauty salons and a personal attack on a local who had fallen out of favor.

I did my best to field the questions directed at me, while listening attentively so I wouldn't lose the thread of the conversation. My comprehension still wasn't stellar, and if I tuned out for a minute I was lost. I looked up words in my dictionary and shared English words with them. These conversations often deteriorated into new slang expressions, and we were amused to no end when someone repeated a vulgar word in the other's language.

"*Testa di cazzo,*" I said each time I saw Caterina.

"Dick 'ed," she'd reply loudly, cracking me up every time.

The stoop belonged to a residential building where two or three people lived. I often saw one fiftyish man who, when not coming and going in a hurry, was busy shouting at some as-yet-unseen person inside whose voice was lost under the thunder of his. No one in the group seemed to think these shouting matches were out of the ordinary.

The only other person from the building I saw frequently was an old woman with short curly hair in a striking blue rinse . . . *capelli blu,* I liked to call it. My grandmother used to wear a similar rinse, and I found it oddly comforting that this old lady fashion statement transcended borders. I had yet to see one beshawled hunched-over old woman, however; you know, the stereotypical *signora* dressed all in black like in every old Italian film as well as in many modern travelogues. I wasn't calling anyone a liar, but the older ladies I'd witnessed were usually wearing skirts and tops and looked pretty put together. There was a regular procession of them around four thirty when the bells chimed their vigorous reminder of Mass at Sant'Agostino.

The old woman in this particular building did sport a shmata, an old housedress and apron, but as she was often coming out to scrub the stoop, I was sure that wasn't her Sunday best. Caterina and the woman, Veda, had an interesting relationship. Whenever Veda came down the street, Caterina went into the cheese shop and brought out a key for her. Veda unlocked the front door of her building and then handed the key back to Caterina. It was the kind of thing you might ask of someone if you'd locked yourself out, but Veda did it almost every day. Maybe she'd lost one too many keys? I'd tried asking Caterina, but her response was too fast and lengthy for me to comprehend—yet another mystery I would one day unlock when my Italian was better.

On my behalf, Caterina had taken to asking everyone and their mother (literally) if they needed help or if they would like to take English lessons. It was so heartwarming, I decided that if I ever had money, I'd take care of Caterina in her old age. After all, she was the first person here who had really gone out of her way to help me.

✦   ✦   ✦

After mentally preparing for another day of job-hunting, I stopped by for a chat with Caterina before heading up to Piazza Grande where there was the slimmest possibility of a restaurant's needing help because a waitress had left to have a baby. Apparently, Pietro told Simone who told Gabriella who mentioned it to Caterina who then told me. Are you getting an idea of how things work here?

I was showered, primped, and I'd taken the precaution of spritzing on an extra dose of perfume to cover up any discernible whiff of failure I might be emitting. I'd even rehearsed how to explain the working *in nero* thing in a way that wouldn't bring on a repeat of Alba's "*schifo*" comment.

While I chatted with Caterina, Veda entered the cheese shop, key in hand.

"This is Jennifer," Caterina told Veda in Italian. "She's looking for work. Do you need any help?"

Veda stared at me for a minute, then nodded slowly. "Yes, I have been looking for someone to help me with my mother and aunt. They are elderly. Both in their nineties."

She spoke rapidly, but I understood that she wanted someone to come in, clean a little, make lunch, and supervise.

I was about say, "I'll take it," when Caterina caught my eye, her expression telling me to wait. Plus, Veda looked a little too eager, her blue head bobbing up and down in anticipation.

"*Posso pensare un pò?*" I politely asked for time to think about it. Caterina then repeated my request in proper Italian so that Veda understood.

"*Qual'è il problema?*" I asked Caterina after Veda was back inside her building.

As I listened, my face fell. The problem was, apparently, that Veda was looking for a servant to bathe, feed, and change the women. When I still wasn't sure I had grasped all of the duties involved, Caterina loudly put it in words I could understand: "*Cacca e pipì.*"

Ahhh! I could clearly see the squalid Dickensian room with the two withered women, bedridden, lacking in daily hygiene and taken care of grudgingly by the overworked Veda. It was hot and dank and smelled of death. I was dressed in my own shmata and now toiled from dawn to dusk à la Cinderella. I thought of the words "*buon stipendio,*" which Caterina had said was the only good thing. It paid well. But when the image zoomed in on my actually trying to change dirty diapers for the old women, I looked at Caterina and began to cry.

"*Non posso,*" I told her. I just didn't have the stomach to do it. Maybe if it was one woman, I could try, but two? Coming out from behind the cheese counter, Caterina held out her arms for a moment before dropping them, wanting to comfort me but unsure what to do. She said something about it taking a special fortitude for that type of work, and I sniffled and agreed that I just wasn't cut out for it. We went outside so Caterina could smoke, and then Antonella came over, wanting to know what was going on. Caterina got her up to date in rapid Italian, and when I heard "*cacca e pipì*" again, I began to really cry. Not just a few tears, but weeks of frustrating job search "why-won't-anyone-hire-me-so-I-don't-have-to-change-old-lady-diapers" tears. Sitting on Veda's stoop I let the tears fall. Niccolò, Silvano, and Giuseppe all emerged from their shops to see what was going on. I realized, as I sat there looking at myself as if I were outside my body, that Italians don't do very well with public displays of emotion. They all stood around awkwardly, not sure where to look. I heard Niccolò say, "*Sta sclerando*," which meant "She's freaking out."

Their responses were even more upsetting than my actual loss of control, so I pulled myself together and walked up the street a little to catch my breath. Giuseppe came over, and, not knowing what to say, asked me to translate a couple of stories about gnomes for his store. I gave him a grateful look and a big hug; he looked so uncomfortable that I began to laugh. I apologized to the gang for my burst of emotion, then endured five minutes of teasing by Caterina and Antonella, telling me they were going to enroll me in *asilo*, which is the preschool.

Really, they needed to work on the empathy thing.

I was puffy-eyed but determined, so I decided to go up to Piazza Grande anyway. Obviously, I had nothing to lose. But I was barely in the door of the restaurant when I learned that the position had already been filled. Probably while Pietro had been telling Simone who told Gabriella, someone farther up in the game of telephone got the jump on me. I headed home depressed, drained, and *abbattuta*. Beaten down.

But even as I crawled onto the sofa and snuggled up with Cinder, I closed my eyes and made myself repeat one thing: If I was going to be homeless, at least I would be homeless . . . in Tuscany.

CHAPTER FIFTEEN

BEWARE OF TUSCANS BEARING GIFTS

Summer had arrived. Sunflowers blanketed nearby fields and temperatures during the day climbed to a hundred degrees. Mercato stands overflowed with peppery arugula, cucumbers, tomatoes, and eggplant, as well as an abundance of peaches, plums, apricots, and watermelon. Daily deliveries of tomatoes and zucchini from Marinella's *orto* inundated my kitchen. The only thing missing was corn, which I'd seen growing on the side of the road, but Marinella informed me it was only used for animal feed. No corn on the cob? That was just wrong.

I was slowly starting to get used to the fact that if it wasn't in season—or like corn, wasn't a staple of the Tuscan diet—I wouldn't find it in grocery stores. If I wanted asparagus in October or a fresh peach in January, forget it. Unlike New York, where I could count on some part of the world cultivating the fruit I wanted whenever I wanted, here it was as the seasons dictated. Menus changed with the arrival of each new fruit or vegetable. Every now and again I'd find something at the mercato that was "out of season," but it wasn't embraced enthusiastically by the locals.

"Those cherries are from South Africa," Marinella would inform me. Nose wrinkle.

Emphasis was placed on local products so much that fruit vendors were especially proud when they could claim their lettuce or arugula or peaches were *nostra produzione*. Our production.

Despite the hot days, the apartment was cool and pleasant, just as Luciana had predicted. Cinder usually hung out in the bathroom, not because the tiles there were any cooler, but because she liked to stalk the flies that occasionally buzzed in and out. Most people in town regularly closed their shutters in the afternoon, but I couldn't bear for the apartment to be so dark. I was told that in addition to protection from the heat of the sun, this habit or tradition of closing the shutters evolved from the time when the shallow waters of the nearby Lago Trasimeno were considered to bring bad air in the summertime, which would make people sick. Closing the shutters ostensibly provided protection from this *mal aria*. The overpopulation of mosquitoes thriving in the lake is more likely what made people sick, though; "malaria" was a fairly serious problem for years. Today, of course, there is no such threat, but people still close their shutters against the midday heat of the sun in an effort to keep the cool air inside.

My normal warm weather morning routine had included some writing time on our porch, but after my laptop and I were pooped on for the umpteenth time by low flying birds, I'd shifted it to afternoons at Serena's bar. I still hoped there was something to the superstition that getting pooped on was good luck.

I'd taken to having an afternoon *shakerato*, an iced espresso made in a shaker and served in a martini glass. It tasted exactly the same as a regular iced espresso but it looked more elegant. I'd put myself on a strict budget, but a daily coffee at the bar was my one extravagance. While I enjoyed a cold drink on a hot day, I was learning that a lot of Italians didn't feel the same way. "*Fa male*," Antonella said when I asked why everyone always drank their beverages at room temperature. "It makes you sick." So a cool drink makes you sick but a frozen gelato is OK? Huh.

When I stopped in at the bar one afternoon, I was just about to order when an older bald man in jogging attire sidled up to me. "*Shakerato, vero?*" He smiled. I couldn't decide if it was nice or creepy that he'd seen me here enough to know my regular drink order.

"Um . . . *sì, grazie*," I said looking around for Serena or Stefano. But the only person working was their employee, Tamara.

"I'm Giorgio," he said, teeth flashing white in a very tanned face. "I've seen you before. Beautiful dog. I live between here and Rome, and I have an apartment in Montepulciano. I sell wine and have other business ventures. My girlfriend left me. How do you like Montepulciano?"

"I like it very much," I said, responding only to the last thing he said. My head spun with how fast he changed subjects.

"Here is my card if you need anything," he said, pushing it into my hand. He leaned in, too close, his breath hot in my ear. "Anything at all."

I swigged the rest of my *shakerato*. "Thanks, it was nice meeting you. Must get Cinder out for a walk. I'm sure we'll see you around."

◆ ◆ ◆

The next day when I entered the bar, Serena beckoned to me. She held up a bottle of wine. "From your admirer," she told me. Then, seeing my dismay, she continued, "Don't worry. Giorgio's harmless. You can consider yourself officially welcomed."

I looked at the wine, which was actually a nice bottle of Vino Nobile, *Riserva*. I read the note out loud. "Looking forward to giving you a proper welcome." Ewww. Why is it always the men you aren't interested in who send the expensive bottles of wine? He left the price tag on too, I noted. Classy.

I sighed. "I'm having this type of week," I told Serena. "First a break down on the *corso* in front of half the town, and then invitations from men who've been shunned by their girlfriends."

As I was walking with Cinder back to our apartment, I saw Giorgio up ahead perched on a bench. Had he been waiting for me?

I resisted the urge to turn around. He waved heartily. "You received my gift?" he asked.

I pointed to the bag in my hand. "Yes, thank you so much."

"Please join me," he said, patting the bench beside him. Sixty-four, divorced twice, Giorgio now went to therapy because of his recent break-up. He relayed all of this in the first thirty seconds. Right. At least my instincts to not encourage him were spot on.

"I don't like to live alone," he continued, barely coming up for air. "But I don't enjoy women who are assertive." He looked me up and down. "You are not so young," he declared.

What was the Italian word for rude?

"Do you like fish?" he asked.

"Well, I—" I began.

"I love it," he interrupted, "but only when it's fresh. And I mean fresh like caught that morning. Not the stuff you find around here."

"*Mi piace*—" I tried again.

"And if you do find something decent here, it's overpriced."

I made one more attempt to speak but then gave up. It was impossible to get a word in edgewise. The Italian name for this, which I learned from Antonella when I told her of my meeting Giorgio, was "*chiacchierone.*" Blowhard. She was well-acquainted with Giorgio's loquaciousness.

"So would you like to come to my house for dinner?" he finished.

I considered his shiny bald head, trying to formulate the appropriately delicate response. But then I considered, too, his comment about my not being so young and threw subtlety out the *finestra*.

"Normally I don't go out with men who are older than my dad," I told him. "He's sixty. You understand; it would just be strange. But if you'd like to be friends, that would be lovely." I flashed a big smile, and then Cinder and I took our leave. He shook my hand and stared after us in silence.

Ecco fatto! I'd succeeded in rendering him speechless.

CHAPTER SIXTEEN

THE AMERICANS ARE COMING

The next week as I lingered outside the cheese shop chatting with Caterina, she waved to a silver-haired dervish of a man whirling up the *corso*.

"Robert, come meet one of your people," Caterina called to the man in Italian. He slowed his pace, the messy pile of papers clutched to his chest threatening to blow away when he shaded his eyes to look at me.

"Another American? Great! We could use reinforcements here."

Short and tanned with ocean-green eyes, Robert thrilled me with the immediately detectable "New York" in his accent.

"I think you might want to request someone who can speak the language a little better. An 'Italian in training' they call me."

He laughed. "That's high praise, actually. As for me, well, I married an Italian, so I have a leg up on the language thing, I'll admit. And now, with four kids I'm definitely here to stay. I've been here over fifteen years now. So what brings you to Montepulciano?"

"A writer looking for inspiration, I guess. That at least is abundant here. Jobs less so."

"Work issues, eh?" Robert asked. He pointed to the pile of papers he held. "I've just come from the employment office. I'm a history teacher, and I teach a class in Perugia. Unfortunately, the university is debating whether to fund it this year."

"That's terrible. I'm not having much luck either." I gave him a twenty-second recitation of my work woes.

Robert shook his head. "It's definitely hard here, but once you get that first job, others will follow."

"Jennifer teaches English and is a very good baker," Caterina told Robert.

"It's true," I said. "I've had a lot of time on my hands, so I've been baking *dolci americani* for the Italians over the last two months and everyone seems to like them."

"What kind of *dolci*?" he asked. "Like apple pie?" His eyes lit up like a kid on Christmas morning.

"I haven't made a pie here yet, but I've made cookies, banana bread, and brownies."

"Mmmm. Brownies. That sounds delicious. I'm soooo not a fan of the Tuscan pastry. It's dry and bland, and everything tastes the same. Have you thought about doing something with the baking?"

We talked about the possibility of baking as a side business, and I felt a tiny glimmer of hope bubbling up inside of me. Baking is a passion for me. In New York, I regularly whipped up brownies, cakes, tarts, lemon bars, banana bread, holiday cookies; if you wanted it, I'd attempt it. Summertime brought strawberry shortcake, peach cobbler, and berry tarts. I'd become so notorious for my baking that friends put in orders for birthdays, Thanksgiving, and requests for their favorite cookies over the holidays.

But baking in Italy was different. They don't even have a word for baking other than *cucinare al forno*, cooking in the oven, so I knew it might be an uphill battle trying to find some of my essential ingredients. While I'd enjoyed some delicious homemade Italian desserts (Antonella makes a scrumptious *panna cotta*), the *pasticcerie*, pastry shops, weren't nearly as good. Lots of pretty cookies and tarts filled their display cases, but they tasted rather similar, or worse, looked better than they tasted.

After my cooking class with Fabio, I knew where to find flour, sugar, good butter, and all of the specialized ingredients for Italian pastries. Chocolate chips were another matter. The brown sugar I finally found was too grainy with a strong molasses odor that refused to "pack" at all, the vanilla was in powder form—and forget buttermilk and sour cream, those didn't even exist in Montepulciano.

Every time I baked here, I'd wrap individual packages for my new friends. As I received more and more positive responses (Antonella even suggested I start my own *pasticceria*), I began to wonder if this was something I could actually do for a living. Robert's putting into words something that had been in the back of my mind seemed like providence.

We chatted for about twenty minutes and during the course of our conversation, three of Robert's friends walked by; I wanted to hug him every time he introduced me as his friend and said I was looking for work.

"Let's definitely stay in touch," Robert said. "I'll have you over so you can meet the family. We live in a little town about ten minutes away."

"That would be lovely," I told him as we exchanged numbers and emails. "And I'll make you that apple pie."

As I watched him walk away, I had to resist the urge to grab onto his shirttails and not let him go. I hadn't realized how much I needed to just talk about my frustrations and worries with a fellow American. To hear the pragmatism of a New Yorker was an added bonus. I felt infinitely better. Here was someone who hadn't had an easy time of it either, but he did it successfully and had been here for over fifteen years. I resolved to explore the baking idea a little more and see if it was a viable option.

❖   ❖   ❖

In other American news, Silvano the butcher had been spreading word that an American family was moving into town. With five children. Even though babysitting as work had potential, I wasn't sure how I felt about their impending arrival. I kind of liked being the only American living in Montepulciano. Other Americans lived nearby, of course, but like Robert, they were outside of town. I was now going to be one of many, it seemed.

Sure enough, late one Sunday afternoon, a large silver minivan inched up the *corso*. Lest you think I was stalking, I should note that the *palazzo* they rented is right across from Antonella's grocery store and only two doors down from "our" stoop, so I couldn't *help* but notice their arrival.

The dad, tall and blond, looking shell-shocked, began unloading a mountain of suitcases and duffle bags from the van, tossing them into the foyer of the *palazzo*. Then out popped kids. Like a clown car, I thought, as white-blond heads kept emerging. I counted them. Yep, five kids. If it were possible, it seemed three were triplets and young ones at that. The mom attempted to hustle all the kids inside like a mother duck corralling her ducklings. Was there a nanny tucked somewhere in the van? I didn't see one. I dug out my cards, entreating Antonella and Caterina to pass them on if the family asked about babysitting help. It didn't occur to me until later that unless the family was fluent in Italian, that scenario wasn't likely to happen.

A few days later, while I was chatting with Antonella and Caterina, the whole family emerged from their building. The boys, four blond boomerangs, began zigzagging across the street and back, yelling and shouting in glee. Their sister remained close to the mom. Heads began craning from nearby windows, curious to see the commotion coming from the street. With Caterina practically pushing me toward them, I took the opportunity to introduce myself.

"Hi, I'm Jenny, the American welcoming committee," I said, approaching the couple. I guessed early-forties, but they radiated youth, looking fit and adorable. "I have no gifts, but if you want to know where to buy the best cheese or what times the shops open and close, I'm your girl."

The woman smiled. "I'm Bonnie," she said. "It's great to hear some English." She glanced around, keeping tabs on the kids as she spoke. I detected the wisp of a southern accent in her words. "Do you live nearby?" With her long straight brown hair and dark eyes, Bonnie stood in stark contrast to the rest of her fair-haired family. She'd dressed up for their outing, wearing a white sundress with thin spaghetti straps that was belted in the middle and showed off her petite figure. Her daughter's dress was a miniature version in pink.

"Just down the street," I told her.

"Mark," said her husband, coming forward to shake my hand formally. Tall, with a pasty complexion, Mark looked as if he spent most days locked inside. He'd checked his iPhone repeatedly in the time he'd been standing there. Suddenly, alarm crossed his face, and he took off running after one of the triplets, who didn't see the orange tour bus hurtling up the street. Mark scooped him up in one fluid motion and headed back toward us.

Bonnie and Mark had been living in Colorado and were moving here to give their family a new experience, one a little less spoiled and a little more worldly. Bonnie didn't seem to need any help with the kids, so I bit my tongue about babysitting.

"We're waiting for our landlords to pick us up for dinner," Bonnie told me, checking her watch. "They invited us to their house. I just hope they know what they are getting into with five small children." I didn't burden them with the "Italian time" conversion, which meant they were going to be waiting for at least another twenty minutes.

I watched as Antonella and Caterina played with the other two triplets, picking them up and swinging them around, laughing at the delighted screams. In just a few short days they had both become favorites with the kids.

We chatted a little bit about our moves to Italy and how out of all the hill towns in all the world, we'd settled on Montepulciano.

"We're planning to stay for a few years," Bonnie said. "The timing seemed right since the little ones are four and just now beginning school."

What did Mark do for work? I wondered. The whole town was dying to know. What he did for a living had been the subject of much debate, overly masticated like a grisly piece of meat, along with how much they must be paying to rent half of a *palazzo*. There were few secrets in this town. And I was under strict orders from Antonella to get the employment scoop.

As I shared with Bonnie some of the things I'd learned by trial and error over the past couple of months including where she could buy a cell phone and the location of the post office, Antonella juggled one of the little ones on her hip. The daughter, Natalie, tugged on Antonella's apron, trying to tell her something.

"Natalie *piace molto il tuo negozio, e anche che tu hai* Gatorade," I said to Antonella, acting as translator so that she understood that Natalie liked her store very much, especially the fact that she stocked Gatorade.

"Your Italian is excellent," Bonnie told me when I'd finished translating. "I've just enrolled at Il Sasso, and my two oldest are going to go there for a few months as well. I hope we will be able to speak as well as you."

"I'm taking lessons there too," I said. I didn't tell her that I'd been studying the language (albeit lackadaisically) for four years because I didn't want to discourage her, but it sounded as if none of them spoke a word of Italian. And I thought I'd had it rough.

When their car finally arrived, or I should say *cars*, as there seemed to be a small fleet pulling up to the *palazzo*, we exchanged phone numbers and emails.

"Mark's going to be out of town next week, so you'll have to come over for a glass of wine, and we'll have a proper chat," Bonnie said as they were leaving.

"That would be fun," I told her. Then my desperation about work forced me to blurt out, "And if you need any help with the kids, I'm happy to help with babysitting."

I headed home feeling better than I had in weeks. I'd been adamant before moving here that I wasn't going to hang out with expats and that I would only speak Italian. I could now see this was neither practical nor conducive to long-term survival. Sure, I would speak mostly Italian, but a "girls' night" every now and again during which I could converse at a normal pace and express everything I wanted to say may be just what I needed to help me feel at home.

CHAPTER SEVENTEEN

MY HILL TOWN'S ALIVE WITH THE SOUND OF MUSIC

A few days later, I got a full dose of what life with five kids was like. When I arrived for our girls' night, Bonnie opened the door, smiling but fatigued. She wore makeup, her big brown eyes expertly done, and her long straight hair was pulled back in a loose pony tail. She sported jeans, a tailored white button-down shirt and was barefoot. She looked young, closer to twenty than forty.

"It's always nuts when Mark is out of town," she explained as she led me up the enormous wide stone steps of the *palazzo*. "Add to that the newness of the place and the difficulty with the language . . ." She laughed. "Well, I don't have to tell you, you've done it too."

"*L'avventura*," we both said at the same time, then laughed. I liked her already.

I could hear excited voices from down the seemingly endless hallway, but they were muffled. This is how the other half lives, I thought as we walked through a cavernous foyer toward the kitchen. Wood paneling halfway up the wall, vaulted ceilings. Was that a *trompe l'oeil*? The furniture was massive and antique. Paintings fifteenth century. It didn't exactly look suited to five rambunctious kids dashing through its salons and playing among its frescoes. I imagined hand-blown vases being toppled with regularity.

Either the massiveness of the *palazzo* had swallowed all of the clutter or Bonnie was running a tight ship. Where were the toys underfoot? The detritus you'd expect from four-year-old triplets?

Bonnie must have seen my incredulity, because she offered, "Our boxes won't be here for at least another month; we have over two hundred coming. Not sure where we're going to put all of our stuff."

Bonnie had already opened a bottle of Vino Nobile and was reaching for the glasses when a scream echoed throughout the *palazzo*.

"It all can go badly very quickly," she said. "Let me just get everyone tucked in once again, and then we'll go up on the terrace."

I'm not sure what wands she waved, but not another peep from the far end of the hall was heard the rest of the evening.

We climbed a narrow wooden staircase to the second story, crossed through a parlor with a cozy fireplace and plush armchairs perfect for tucking up your feet and settling down to read, and then up another even narrower flight to the terrace. The view of nearby Lago Trasimeno and Cortona in the fading light of the day was splendid.

"The only thing missing is the sunset," she said. "We have the eastern view."

"You're welcome to come over to my place whenever you have a sunset craving," I told her. "I don't have a terrace, but there's a lovely broken down bench that has a bit of charm."

"Sounds perfect."

Over the next three hours, we reclined on lounge chairs, stared at the starry sky, and hit the highlights on our life stories. We worked our way through not one, but two bottles of wine.

"My new Italian friends would be scandalized," I said, getting up to peer over the edge of the terrace at Antonella and Caterina's stores. Caterina had gone home, but Antonella's lights were on. Since it was summer, she was surely in the back reading a juicy novel, open late in case anyone had a prosciutto or *pane* emergency. "They usually don't drink unless they're eating a meal, and then only a glass . . . maybe two."

"More for us," Bonnie said, holding up her glass, and we cracked up. It was like hanging out with Cheryl, comfortable and fun.

After hearing about some of my funnier escapades in Montepulciano, including launching my body out of my window to singlehandedly replace the laundry line, Bonnie readily volunteered to help on the job front by admitting she could use some help with the kids.

"They're all potty-trained," she told me with a mischievous laugh. "No changing diapers required." I shuddered, thinking of my narrow escape from the two old ladies.

"Even if they weren't, I'd take it in a minute. Your kids are great."

And I meant that, albeit in the abstract. Because in fact, I hadn't spent much time with them yet. They were all in bed tonight, or at least in their rooms, so it wasn't until Bonnie invited me to go to dinner with them the next night that I really experienced them.

Beginning the following night, Montepulciano would kick off its first big event of the summer, the XXXIV Cantiere Internazionale d'Arte di Montepulciano, an annual music festival that lasts throughout July. Alberto had already burst my bubble about getting a few hours' work there when he told me that they wouldn't hire off the books.

"But what about ticket takers? Surely they need people to do some menial jobs like that."

"Yes," he'd responded, "but unfortunately this event is well-established, and they aren't going to hire anyone *in nero* . . . even for the menial jobs." His tone was apologetic, but at this point I was holding him responsible for my lack of work, and my crush had faded like last season's poppies. Too many people had wondered, "Why isn't Alberto helping you?" and I was forced to agree. Why *wasn't* he doing more to help? He owned half the town, and he knew everyone. I was also angry at myself for spending way more money than I should have to prolong my Italian lessons all because of a stupid crush. It was unreasonable to blame my troubles on Alberto, but at that moment all I kept thinking was that my Quinty hadn't lived up to expectations. He didn't even mix me drinks.

When I met Bonnie and her gang in front of their building, the kids were literally dancing with excitement. A band, who would later play in Piazza Grande, snaked its way up the *corso*. Henry, the most outgoing triplet, greeted me by jumping into my arms and asking me to carry him up the hill. The others ran ahead, forcing Bonnie and me to try to keep tabs on the bobbing blond heads skipping along behind the drummers.

"At least there's no traffic," Bonnie said cheerfully. "Remind me to tell you about when Kyle jumped off a moving train."

"Um, OK." The kids were getting kind of far ahead of us, and I lost sight of two. I wasn't feeling her calm, let-them-get-the-energy-out-before-dinner vibe. It had only been three minutes, and I was feeling a nonplussed, oh-shit-how-does-she-keep-track-of-all-of-them vibe coupled with an I-hope-I-don't-have-a-heart attack-before-we-get-to-restaurant feeling. Was this a test to see how I'd be as a babysitter? I hoped I got points for the carrying part. With Henry weighing me down, I was feeling the burn. While I had lots of experience handling large numbers of dogs in New York, happily walking five or six at a time, I didn't have as much experience with multiple kids. I anxiously tried to track blond heads as the growing crowd carried us forward.

Would it be wrong to suggest leashes?

When the band veered up a side street, I felt no small amount of relief. We were just steps away from the restaurant . . . Alberto's restaurant. In a strange coincidence, when I was getting ready earlier in the evening, the manager of Alberto's restaurant called—the one who, three months ago, hadn't seemed convinced I could handle the job. He asked if I could work because two of his servers were out sick. My elation was momentary. I was sure Alberto hadn't informed him that I now was hampered by my paperwork problem. Rather than go into a long history, I just told him I couldn't, but that I was having dinner at the restaurant, and I would try to speak to him then. Since Alberto had made it clear he didn't want to take the risk of my working there, there was no point in dwelling on the irony of a work opportunity presenting itself on the one night I had plans I couldn't cancel for fear of missing out on another work opportunity.

I hadn't seen Alberto in over a week because Il Sasso was overrun with students at this time of year, and he couldn't fit me in for a lesson. He greeted me with his usual warmth, and I told him about his manager's call. He said he'd speak with him. He did not, however, say he'd be calling again.

I hadn't eaten in a restaurant since I'd moved to Italy. I didn't enjoy eating in restaurants alone, and the few times I'd made plans with Laura or Antonella they'd had to cancel. But if I'd thought I might actually be enjoying a peaceful meal tonight, I realized after minute one that it wasn't likely to happen. Bonnie ordered us a bottle of Brunello, a wine I loved, but it was expensive and meant I was going to blow my budget for the week.

There was no way to order courses with all the kids. All you could hope for was that the five pizzas arrived quickly before the remarkably good behavior began to wane. Since Mark was away, Zack took the head spot at the table. At eight, he was the oldest and very smart.

"I eat Nutella every day now," he told me when the kids were volunteering their favorite foods in Italy.

When I commented that it seemed like an awful lot of Nutella, he informed me that it was just like having peanut butter only with hazelnuts. I had to remember that rationalization. I'd always thought of Nutella as a decadent chocolate treat, but in reality Zack was right. It's a hazelnut spread (with some cocoa); its ingredients were probably no worse than commercial peanut butter.

Other than Zack, I chatted most with Henry and Natalie, who were seated on either side of me. Natalie and I discovered that both our birthdays were coming up the following week.

"We're going to Gardaland," she told me proudly as she wiggled one of her teeth, which was loose.

Gardaland is Italy's answer to Disneyland and, as the name implies, is situated near Lake Garda, a few hours north of Montepulciano.

"That's pretty great," I told her.

"Yeah," said little Henry, who was now sitting on my lap. "It's going to be way fun." Then he added, "I love you, Jenny."

Beaming, I helped cut pizza for as many kids as I could reach and watched as Henry methodically ate a huge plate of French fries. I scarfed down some pizza and sipped my wine, trying to ignore the pointed looks from the diners seated around us as the volume at our table rose.

Get used to it, I thought. They're here to stay.

Bonnie seemed tired but perked up after a few glasses of wine. She insisted on paying for dinner, so I treated everyone to gelato on the way home. The kids were already regulars at the *gelateria*, and the cute young owner, Vincenzo, obligingly scooped their *piccole* (small) cups of *stracciatella* (Italian chocolate chip) and *vaniglia*, smiling broadly as they said "*Grazie.*" As the kids slowly marched toward home in high spirits, spooning up their rapidly melting ice cream, I couldn't help feeling like Maria in *The Sound of Music* as I trailed along behind them.

Bonnie booked me for a night of babysitting the following week, and we shared hugs all around as we said *buona notte.*

Natalie pulled me aside. "I hope we can have some girl time when you come," she told me. "It's not easy being the sister of four brothers." She looked around, then lowered her voice. "They are out to destroy me," she confided with a dramatic sigh.

"I will definitely see what I can do about girl time," I promised. "And maybe I can make you something special for your birthday."

"Anything chocolate," she told me. I smiled, nodding in approval.

We were going to get along just fine.

CHAPTER EIGHTEEN

L'AVVOCATO

The lawyer walked into my life—and Serena's bar—with the slow swagger of a cowboy in a western. The afternoon sun cast a shadow across the floor of the bar, and all I could see initially was a tall figure in white straddling the doorway. The theme music from *The Good, the Bad, and the Ugly* briefly flitted through my brain.

As he crossed out of the shadows and was revealed totally, I saw that he was an ordinary man, dressed head to toe in white linen. Hair as white as his clothing flowed like a lion's mane. Robust with a bit of a paunch, he swayed a little as he made his way deliberately to the bar, and I realized, Hey! You're swaggering because you're tipsy. Evidently there were some exceptions to the one glass of wine with a meal theory.

I stood at the bar, sipping a *shakerato* and keeping a short leash on Cinder, who was eagerly eyeing a young kid with a drippy cone of chocolate gelato. I told Serena about the babysitting assignment Bonnie had scheduled.

"It's a start," she offered encouragingly.

When the lawyer literally bellied up to the bar, Serena introduced me as her American friend. Piercing blue eyes attempted to focus in on me. And then, with a grand wave of welcome, the lawyer did what a lot of the men here did when they heard I was American: he spoke two halting sentences in English to let me know he could. When I heard his name I thought it sounded familiar. My eyes moved slowly to two bottles of wine behind the bar. Oh. Got it. Both his Vino Nobile and Vino Rosso had prominent places on the shelf. I remembered Serena telling me that *un avvocato*, or a lawyer, had started a winery a few years ago. Turned out I wasn't the only one who'd gotten fed up with practicing law. Of course, I didn't have the money to buy a vineyard and start an agriturismo, but other than that we were practically soul mates.

"*Prendi un caffé?*" he asked, switching back into Italian, asking me if I wanted a coffee. I was about to tell him I just had one when I noticed Serena motioning me to accept. She'd removed my glass and had already grabbed the shaker to start a new one.

"Yes, thanks," I said.

Surprisingly, instead of a cocktail the lawyer requested an orange juice and a *panino*. As we had our drinks, he asked me about my move to Italy and patted Cinder, who was utterly devoted to him after he tossed her a piece of his sandwich. She'd developed a proprietary air at the bar and now had no qualms about staring down unsuspecting customers who were having their morning brioche or afternoon bar snacks. And not offering any to her.

I told him the short version of my move, leaving out the *schifo*, tears, and frustration. He asked what I'd like to do, and I mentioned perhaps working in a restaurant or *enoteca*. I didn't have the *palle* to discuss the working *in nero* thing.

"She makes delicious desserts," Serena added.

"You like to cook. *Brava*. It's normally not difficult to find work here, but this is a slow year. But let me think about this, and I'll see if I can find something for you.

"Our agriturismo is just down the road. You'll have to come out, and I will show you around. And you must meet my daughter. She was also a lawyer, but no longer practices."

We shared a conspiratorial laugh at our mutual dissatisfaction with the legal profession. It was almost an epidemic.

"I would love to meet your daughter and see the property," I said, handing him my card. "Here's my number."

He tucked the card into his breast pocket and patted it. "I will call you in a few days."

"Great. Thank you for the coffee." After he left, I turned to Serena, beaming. "First babysitting and now another possible job opportunity. I feel like I'm about to jump out of my skin."

"Nah. That's the double dose of caffeine you just had," she said deadpan. "Aren't you glad you stayed? I have a good feeling about this."

I didn't want to get my hopes up, but I couldn't help feeling a little lighter as I made my way back along the ancient bricked streets.

✦   ✦   ✦

Days went by, and I didn't hear from the lawyer. Finally he told Serena he'd stop by the bar on Tuesday morning at ten to take me out to his agriturismo to talk about work options. I was elated. I baked banana bread for him and was dressed and ready right on time. By eleven thirty he still hadn't showed. I left the banana bread at the bar with Serena.

The next day when I was walking Cinder, I ran into *l'avvocato* in the parking area outside the main gate.

P.S. Yes, it is entirely normal for Italians to refer to people by their professions, such as "The Lawyer" or "The Architect."

"I'm sorry I couldn't make it yesterday," he said as I stood there, clutching a bag of dog poop.

"Thank you for the delicious banana cake. We must try again. Maybe next week."

My one job lead seemed to be slipping away.

I'd been here over three months, had only one babysitting job lined up, and everyone had told me how bleak the employment situation was in winter. The unspoken sentiment seemed to be "if you haven't found a job by now, you're screwed." I felt like I was starring in a reverse production of Dante's *Divina Commedia*: I'd begun in *Paradiso*, had worked my way into *Purgatorio*, and now it seemed was on the fast track to Hell. *Inferno*, here I come.

I moped around for a few days. Why was everything so hard here? I made frequent calls to my parents and Cheryl and Will. Hearing their voices helped, but I knew their lives were proceeding apace without me. I wrote a little on my blog, but I purposely kept the tone light and didn't express the panic I'd been feeling. I was pretty confident no one was going to feel sorry for me. I was in Tuscany after all. My readers wanted to hear about wine, romance, and food, not that I was making hard choices between buying groceries or buying tampons in order to stretch my cash. I was eating a lot of tuna sandwiches, so I was probably going to start losing my faculties to mercury poisoning, but what made it all the more torturous was that I didn't enjoy the bread.

Where was the wheat bread? Yes, admittedly this was slightly irrational, and I didn't want to be one of those expats who bitched about missing their favorite American products, but I truly missed healthy bread. The unsalted, hard as a rock, white bread that the Tuscans proudly extoll was not appealing to me. And if I did buy some and didn't eat it the first day, it morphed into a weapon suitable for battle.

I never mentioned my dislike of the bread to Antonella, but surely she wondered why I was her only regular customer who didn't get their daily loaf. One of the old women who came into the store each morning seemed to particularly enjoy the hard bread, always asking for a loaf that was *lungo e duro* (long and hard). This of course would send Antonella and me into convulsions as we struggled to hold back laughs. It was made even more funny by the fact that the woman seemed to have no idea why we thought it amusing, and after she'd leave, we would explode in a fit of juvenile hysterics.

Around this time, I ran into one of my English-speaking neighbors and mentioned my craving for healthy bread. Janet was Australian and her husband English. They were permanent residents, here for over twenty years, according to Marinella. Our windows both faced onto the parking area, and I'd been smiling at Janet whenever we'd pass on the street for months, but she'd never said hello to me. Other than hearing some creative cursing when she'd slipped while hanging out her "bloody" laundry, she had been steadfastly reserved. The consensus from my Italian neighbors was that she was *altezzosa*, the Italian equivalent of snobbish.

But a couple of days earlier, as I was climbing the shortcut into town, I'd seen Janet ahead of me. Mid-sixties with pretty honey-colored hair, she always dressed in skirts and flowing linen blouses, designed no doubt to de-emphasize her enormous chest. I was sure that when she was younger, she'd had the form of a gorgeous pin-up girl.

She'd walked slowly up the hill, her carriage painfully proper, taking the outer edge of the road which is a tad shallower. Perhaps because I no longer cared about being impertinent, I sped up the inside track, overtook her, introduced myself, and forced her into a conversation.

"I live a few houses down from you," I told her, trying to catch my breath a little.

"I've seen you," she said, "but I thought maybe you were just here for the summer. Most of the people who rent Luciana's apartment are tourists."

"No, I'm here for the foreseeable future. I hope for good, but my optimism is waning with the job situation here."

Janet's manner thawed at this disclosure. She stopped and smiled. "Don't get discouraged. It took me three years before I made some income. Even now while I have some English students, the work isn't steady. I do lots of bits and pieces."

We chatted for a couple minutes about our backgrounds, and she told me about her husband. "He's a painter," she said. "I'm here because of him. He's twenty years my senior, and it was his dream to live here." I resisted the urge to ask if he frequented Auser, the pensioners' club we'd just passed on our way up the hill.

Janet spoke almost entirely in English, but I noticed that when she said a few phrases in Italian, I could barely understand her with her heavy Australian accent. She'd been here twenty years. Would I still sound so foreign after living here so long? Would I never shake this unmistakable American accent?

I'd seen Janet a few times since then, usually as we hung out of our respective windows dealing with the laundry. She always waved or called a friendly hello.

And this morning, as Cinder and I were returning from our early morning tour of the mercato, she stopped me to ask how the job hunt was going. I groaned, and she laughed.

"I did find peanut butter at the Conad yesterday," I told her, proud of my supermarket success. "That was the highlight of my week. I'm going to make some peanut butter cookies for my friend's children I've been babysitting. Now if I could just find some decent bread, I'll be happy. I'm thinking about making my own. I really miss whole grain bread."

"Do you not like the bread at the *forno*?" Janet asked, surprised. "I find their *pane integrale* to be quite good."

The *forno* she was referring to is the bread bakery on the main street. I'd been in there a few times but had never seen anything remotely resembling whole wheat bread.

"You have to ask for it," she told me, seeing my doubt. "It's in the back."

I thanked her and stopped in at the *forno* later that day. Only the large white "normal" loaves stared back at me. Smiling, I tentatively asked for the *pane integrale*. The robust woman behind the counter nodded.

"Janet was just here, and she let me know you'd be coming." I knew I shouldn't have been surprised that Janet got there before me, but the workings of a small town never ceased to amaze me. The woman stood there for a moment, assessing me, and I wondered if I was supposed to give a password. It felt very covert, as if it were the secret shame of some Tuscans to admit they didn't like their famous bread. The woman brought out two wonderfully dark loaves, telling me in rapid Italian what was in each. I didn't understand at all, but one looked like rye and the other multigrain.

"I'll take both." I practically sang the words in my excitement. I returned home with the triumph of a hunter who had captured some elusive game. My funk of the past few days lifted, and not even the sound of the daily grunting from next door was enough to dampen my spirits as I buttered and munched on the delicious bread.

Finding the bread was a sign that I just needed to hang on, that whatever I needed would somehow appear.

CHAPTER NINETEEN

TANTI AUGURI A ME!

After a few months in Montepulciano, I was still the only person with bunched up fitted sheets hanging on the line. The only person with red bath towels. The only person who exercised her dog and brought her everywhere. The only person who crunched into an apple without peeling it first.

But despite the ups and downs, I'd also learned many things. I knew that Tuscans went to "the sea" (*il mare*) not to "the beach" in August and that a lot of places were shut up tight for most of that month. I knew that when the church bells gave one solemn chime, someone had died. I knew that the bookstore only received one shipment of titles in English each year, forcing me to peruse the same books every week like a fool repeatedly opening the refrigerator hoping to find something new and exciting on the next pass. I knew that everything from television programming to the theater took meal time into consideration so that films and performances routinely began late in the evening. (An afternoon espresso helps condition you for this.) I'd learned that you don't ask someone "What are you doing *tonight*?" but instead must say "this evening," or you'll be given a look that implies you're a pervert trying to pry into their nighttime activities. I knew that you "took" an appointment and a decision, but "made" a class and a party.

And I knew that whomever had organized the supermarket had a strange sense of humor. Baby food was located next to the liquors, helpful for that mom on the go who just needs a nip to get through the day. Feminine products were alongside the cleaning supplies and garbage bags. Squid was shoved up next to the ice cream, and unless there is some Tuscan specialty called *calamari à la mode* that I don't know about, I found that one to be the oddest.

I'd also discovered if I were looking for some non-Italian item like pickles or ketchup, a low shelf was my best bet, where they'd likely be gathering dust. More for me!

So with all my new-found knowledge and budding friendships, I was slowly weaving myself into the fabric of Montepulciano life—when along came Birthday Week.

Natalie had invited me to her birthday dinner, so I entered Alberto's restaurant for the pizza festivities laden with chocolate cupcakes with pink vanilla icing. The kids ran over, hugging and chanting my name. Mark had returned from the States and seemed a little unsettled at how enthusiastically his kids greeted me. During our evening of babysitting, we'd bonded over cookies and story time; they now treated me like a minor celebrity.

Bonnie poured the wine, Mark and the little ones ate pizza and fries, and I gave my gift to Natalie. She excitedly unwrapped the red leather purse I'd found at Gabriella's shop.

"Every girl needs a real Italian handbag," I told her. She considered this for a moment, nodded happily, then put it over her shoulder and proceeded to wear it everywhere for the next couple of weeks.

For my own birthday a few days later, I didn't have a plan. Bonnie and the kids were off to Gardaland, so I decided to hang out with Serena at the bar in the afternoon. I let a few people know I'd be there, but most of my new friends were working so I wasn't counting on anyone joining me. Birthday celebrations didn't seem to be a priority here. I'd also recently learned that to wish someone "*Buon Compleanno*" (Happy Birthday) or "*Auguri*" (Best Wishes) before their birthday was bad luck. I'd unknowingly done this one time only to have the person look at me as if I'd just assured them a quick trip to the netherworld. The Italians were equally superstitious about baby showers, apparently. The very idea of having a party before the baby's birth was unheard of, I was told. The old superstition says that well-wishers are not even supposed to buy anything for the baby until after it arrives, which I imagine makes for a very chaotic homecoming from the hospital as new parents scramble to secure car seats and cribs. I should note that some crafty expectant parents have found a loophole to this superstition, having *nonna* and *nonno* buy stuff and store it at their house until after the birth.

My birthday superstitions were limited to making a wish when I blew out my candles each year. But I did have a birthday tradition: carrot cake. I had almost given up on the idea for this year. The cake has a decadent cream cheese frosting, and . . . well, you're not likely to find Philadelphia cream cheese in Italy, right? Much to my surprise, it was the easiest of all the "non-Italian" ingredients to find. It's in even the smallest grocery store, and it's simply known as "Philadelphia."

Coconut and buttermilk were the real challenges. I couldn't find buttermilk, so I improvised with lemon juice in milk to make the acidity. The manager at the supermarket told me they didn't have shredded coconut, but as I was making one last pass around the store, on the very bottom shelf in the section with the nuts, I found it. Flaked and perfect. I resisted the urge to find the manager and show him, since I was now a grown-up of thirty-nine years.

The morning of my birthday was hot. It was forecast to reach the upper nineties, which goes with the territory when you have an August birthday. One year in New York, my birthday gathering in the park saw the mercury hit one hundred two degrees. You know you have good friends when they are willing to risk melting faster than the ice in their margaritas in order to celebrate with you.

I set about chopping walnuts, grating carrots, and crushing pineapple for the carrot cake. The familiar act of making my traditional birthday cake in my new country somehow bridged another chasm I hadn't realized needed crossing and brought with it an enormous sense of comfort. The one concession I made to my new life was to make cupcakes instead of a full cake so I could more easily share with everyone.

I loaded up a basket with my cupcakes and headed off like Little Red Riding Hood going to Grandma's. I heard Marinella talking to one of the kitties as I approached her gate. The jasmine cloaking her wall wasn't as intense now with only a few white blooms remaining, but there was still a divine fragrance when I drew near. She added a new plant to the wall each year, and the jasmine was slowly snaking its way around the perimeter. I wondered if eventually we'd be choking on the heady odor instead of enjoying its sweet scent, as the walls slowly suffocated beneath the entwining vines.

Still in her nightgown and robe, Marinella walked around her garden sprinkling flowers with a large watering can.

"*Dolci?*" she called, shaking her head indulgently when she saw me at the gate. "*Sono ingrassata.*" She was joking that I was making her fat, which wasn't true as she looked great. She sunbathed in the afternoons in shorts and a bra; I should only hope to look as good as she did in twenty years.

"*Non è vero,*" I told her, giving her enough cupcakes for the whole family. Marinella often brought me little jelly jars filled with her homemade ragù, or a plate of *crostini* that she'd prepared for a luncheon, so it was fun to surprise her with something from my kitchen.

"Wait here," she told me, setting the watering can on a step and unlatching the gate so I could come inside. "I'll be right back."

She reemerged from her house with two bags, one small and beribboned and the other large and brown with green, leafy carrot tops sticking out of the top.

"*Buon Compleanno,*" she told me, smiling widely.

"From your *orto*?" I asked excitedly, pointing to the vegetables.

"*Sì,*" she said. "Tomatoes, zucchini, carrots, and just for my American friend, two ears of corn. My uncle thought I was crazy when I told him you wanted to eat it. He grows it for the animals."

I poked my head in the bag, excitedly examining the two beautifully yellow ears of corn, inhaling deeply the aroma of the perfectly ripened red tomatoes. I knew she'd picked everything last night and had even troubled to clean off the soil.

"And this?" I asked, already unwrapping the box inside the other bag. A citrusy shower gel was revealed.

"This one," she said, "is because I remembered you'd said you don't like strong perfumes. This is light and fragrant, like the lemons of Capri."

My throat choked with emotion as I hugged her tight. "*Grazie.* You've made my birthday very special."

I gathered up the bags and made my way along the ancient brick street to Janet's house. She invited me in, and I had an opportunity to look around her gorgeously renovated apartment, which covered two floors plus an attic studio where Ken did his painting. I could hear his whistling from upstairs so imagined him hard at work on one of his oil paintings, beautiful depictions of the Tuscan countryside. The tune he whistled was always the same, the almost funereal sounding theme from *Brideshead Revisited.*

Janet had my dream kitchen complete with marble countertops and a professional-looking mixer in stainless steel. I thanked her again for the *pane integrale* tip and dropped off a couple of cupcakes. She wore a bright red apron, had tucked her blonde hair back into two gold combs, and was in the midst of putting together a delicious looking antipasto platter. Her dining table was elegantly set. She told me she was preparing lunch for some visiting friends.

"I'm glad you stopped by," she said. "Marco Ercolani might have work for you when your paperwork is done. Probably in the *enoteca.* I mentioned you to him the other day."

"Thanks. I'm not sure it's going to be anytime soon, but I'll definitely stop in and see him." I wasn't so keen on working for the Pulcino empire, which Janet herself described as an octopus whose tentacles reached everything, but at this point I couldn't afford to be choosy. I had, of course, been in to see Marco twice already, and he hadn't been encouraging. In fact, he'd been one of the people who'd asked why Alberto wasn't helping me.

By the time I climbed the hill into the town, I was perspiring. Definitely a scorcher. I hoped my deodorant held out. Italian deodorant didn't include an antiperspirant, so I made a mental note to add "deodorant" to the care package wish list I'd been compiling for my mom like a kid at summer camp.

The cool air of Caterina's cheese shop was a welcome respite. Like most of the buildings in Montepulciano, the shop didn't have air conditioning, but the ancient stone walls kept it cave-like cool. Caterina was busy with a group of tourists from the States—Georgia or Tennessee, judging from the syrupy accents. They argued about which cheeses they could bring back in their suitcases. A seasoned cheese transporter myself, I showed them which ones they could have vacuum-packed, then chatted with them while Caterina put their order together. One of the men in the group provided the comic relief, making jokes about how much his wife was spending in all of the stores.

"We're doing Tuscany on a thousand euros a day," he told me. They departed after spending over a hundred euros on cheese.

When the store emptied, I gave a cupcake to Caterina, waiting while she tried it. I scanned the cheeses trying to decide between my usual *pecorino con pepe nero* and a cheese Alberto had turned me on to called *peconzola*. A tangy amalgamation of pecorino and gorgonzola, it was my newest addiction. The pecorino cut the strength of the gorgonzola rendering it a little less pungent and a little more *delizioso*. Caterina had suggested putting it over hot pasta, so I'd tried it that way. It was good, but my favorite way to prepare it was crumbled over a salad of arugula with apples or pears.

"*Buonissimo*," Caterina told me as she savored each bite of the cupcake. I'd wanted her to taste it before trying to explain what was in it, which included the tropical ingredients pineapple and coconut as well as the carrots and walnuts. The words *carrot cake*, while sounding perfectly normal to my ears, were strange to an Italian. *Una torta con le carote?* Antonella had been flummoxed when I'd initially mentioned it.

Caterina made my cheese decision for me, presenting me with a piece of the *peconzola* as a birthday gift and followed me up to Antonella's, still raving about the cupcake. Whew. My *dolce americano* was a success. Because if it hadn't been, they would have told me. Caterina and Antonella had no trouble letting me know my lemon bars were slightly too tart for their taste, and Marinella had informed me that my cinnamon buns also weren't sweet enough. "*Mi piace i miei dolci dolci,*" she told me. "I like my dessert sweet." I was starting to get used to the frankness of the Italians when it came to anything food-related, but I'll admit it still stung a little whenever they found fault with something. Thankfully, I wasn't alone in this. Janet, a very good cook, told me about her Italian friends who'd insulted her sweet and sour chicken and only picked at their dinner.

"They don't want to try anything new," she said. "Needless to say, I didn't invite them over again."

Antonella sampled her cupcake, licking the frosting slowly, wanting to identify what was in it. The upside of cooking for these Italians was that they did appreciate everything you put into a recipe. Both women had tortured themselves trying to figure out all the ingredients in the lemon bars, and I thought Antonella was going to go crazy with the carrot cake, struggling to identify all the tastes she was experiencing.

She licked the frosting again. Finally I told her that it was "Philadelphia," reaching into her refrigerator case and pulling out a little packet of Philadelphia cream cheese. "*Come questo.*"

She didn't believe me and took another bite. I took this as success.

+   +   +

After I finished delivering the rest of my cupcakes, the afternoon was a blur of prosecco. First Serena made me some concoction with Campari and prosecco, then I lost count of the glasses I consumed. The Italian word that corresponds with tipsy is *allegra*; when you are three sheets to the wind, you are *ubriaca*. I was somewhere between.

I sat outside, under an umbrella that provided a little shade but not much relief from the blazing sun. I relaxed and let the sun and the prosecco melt me into a puddle of contentment. Tourists streamed by on their way into town, and locals popped in and out of the bar. Many glasses were bought for me, contrary to Italian tradition by which the birthday girl or boy usually buys all the drinks, but hey, sometimes being a *straniera* has its privileges. *Salute!*

Whenever there was a lull, Serena would come out and join us. Cinder, too, had a blast, and at last count, she'd consumed three bowls of water, a discarded ice cream cone, half a tuna sandwich, and a whole tray of bar snacks that fell on the ground. She didn't even mind that the Italians called her "Cenerentola," Italian for Cinderella. I'd used it once to explain her name, and it stuck. As long as there were snacks about, she'd answer to anything.

I was just getting ready to head home when the lawyer saw me and waved heartily. He scraped back a chair at the table next to me and plopped down, seeming as *allegro* as I.

"What are we drinking?" he asked cheerfully, then grimaced when I described the concoction Serena had prepared.

"*Due prosecco,*" he said to Serena. "No red stuff." He toasted me. "*Salute.*" He entertained me with a story of some guests at the agriturismo, charming as always. I sipped the cool bubbly prosecco, enjoying conversing with him, although honestly I didn't understand everything he was saying as he spoke quickly.

"I have an idea," he told me. "I'm thinking about starting a cooking school for my guests at the agriturismo. How would you like to work with an Italian chef and prepare traditional Tuscan dishes? I already know you can cook. That cake you made was wonderful. And you could provide the translation for the English-speaking students."

I tried to be nonchalant, but I wanted to kiss him. "That sounds like a brilliant idea," I told him. It was basically my dream job, so I didn't want to get my hopes up. I told him about how I had done that for Il Sasso and that I'd worked with a chef named Fabio.

"I'll arrange a meeting with the chef I have in mind in a week or two. I'd like to get it up and running by October, but first I have to get through the grape harvest. You are welcome to be on my squad if you want to participate."

"Absolutely," I said, having no idea what was involved in the vendemmia, the annual grape harvest, but I knew that it was a big deal. If I hadn't found steady work by late September, I was sure I'd be up for anything.

Serena wandered out as the lawyer was leaving. "*L'avvocato* just paid your tab," she told me.

I yelled my thanks after him as he headed to his car.

"*Buon Compleanno*," he replied and tipped his hat. There was that cowboy again, this time riding off into the sunset. Happy Birthday indeed. Things were finally looking up.

CHAPTER TWENTY

ENGLISH LESSONS

The dining room was, in a word, elegant. Two mahogany-framed casement windows were open, allowing a late summer breeze to drift into the room. Between them sat an ornate walnut sideboard laden with silver serving pieces and a magnificent vase of hand-blown glass grape clusters. Antique breakfronts graced two walls, appearing to shimmer in the reflection of two crystal chandeliers whose light danced off the highly polished silver pieces within. The table was grand enough to seat twelve and was draped in a flowing creamy linen that reminded me of a wedding gown, heavy with embroidered detail. In addition to the silken napkins and plethora of shining silver, each place had its own crystal pitcher for water and a tiny salt shaker.

I was unaccountably nervous.

I spied a crystal toothpick holder next to the sterling wine coasters and let out a breath. Seeing toothpicks on this lavish table somehow calmed me. I was nervous—not because I'd never had a fancy dinner before, but because of with whom I was dining and what it meant.

My hosts would be the family who owns Poliziano, one of the most important vineyards in Montepulciano. It was the grown-up equivalent of winning the golden ticket to meet Willy Wonka because Poliziano doesn't just make wine . . . they make my *favorite* wine.

When Robert (the American I'd met the month before) called to say he wanted to refer some friends for English lessons, I was over the moon. When he told me who they were, my heart started to race.

"Like . . . the wine?" I'd asked, not daring to hope. Poliziano was the nickname of fifteenth-century humanist poet Angelo Ambrogini, who was born in Montepulciano and who was called Il Poliziano by the Medici family's Lorenzo the Magnificent. People native to Montepulciano are known as Poliziani because the original Latin name for Montepulciano was Mons Politianus, and they are very proud that Il Poliziano was born in their town. His name has been appropriated by more than one establishment; there is a Caffè Poliziano in town too.

"Yes, the wine. Anna has two kids and wants them to become fluent in English. She's willing to pick you up each week and take you to their house for the lessons." I found myself unable to respond.

"Hello? *Pronto?* Are you there?"

"Um, yeah, I'm here. That sounds great."

And now I was *here*. I'd somehow managed to resist jumping out of my centuries-old walnut chair to blurt out my love of their wine and the fact that Cheryl and I drank it as often as we could find it in New York. Or that we'd toured their cellars on our trip a few years ago.

I was seated next to Maria Stella, aged nine, and across from her brother, Francesco, who was eleven but wanted me to know that he'd be twelve in two months. They were relaxed and comfortable. Federico was at the head of the table. He was the force behind Poliziano, the winery his father began over fifty years ago.

"I don't like to speak English at home," he told me. "I must speak it most of the day for work. But Anna wants to do this." Both his brusque manner and his tall, robust physical appearance intimidated me. Tanned and bald, there was evidence of some sort of skin graft on his forehead, which I tried not to stare at, all the while wondering what happened.

"Ignore him," Anna said, warm and down to earth. "I think it is important for the children to learn English. And the English in the schools here is not good.

I think if we have lessons once a week and speak English at dinner, this will be a good introduction. I want them to enjoy learning the language." I studied the kids, who didn't seem to understand any of what Anna was saying. Her English was the best I'd heard in my time here, and she told me it was because she spent her summers in England as a teenager. I learned that Francesco and Maria Stella had just spent their summer holiday in Switzerland where they'd had their first real introduction to learning English. They responded with a few well-practiced phrases, but I could see we would have some work to do.

I kept waiting for Anna or Federico to grill me about my background, but neither seemed concerned about my qualifications. Either Robert's recommendation was enough or maybe Bonnie had said some nice things about me. I knew Bonnie had spoken to Anna earlier in the week because as it turns out, Bonnie's *palazzo* was owned by Anna's family. They make wine too. In fact, they've been making it a lot longer than Poliziano, but their operation is small and run completely by women: Anna, her mom, and her sister. Villa Sant'Anna is named for her, and she and Federico have a good-natured competition about their respective winemaking enterprises. I noted that the bottle we were drinking was Federico's.

As we ate a first course of *crostini* with smoked salmon, I had to constantly remind myself to speak in English after months of trying to say everything in Italian. A gray-haired woman with kind eyes served the meal, and when I saw that the main course was spare ribs, I had a moment of Eliza Doolittle-like panic. I was actually well-versed in table etiquette thanks to parents who enjoyed dining in posh places, but after seeing the Italians peel even their fruit with a knife, I was curious if they'd eat their ribs with their fingers.

They did.

They were so normal that the contrast between the luxury in which we were dining and the informality of the people felt strange. The fact that they had a cook and a nanny and were being served their meal was in sharp contrast to the relaxed mannerisms and lighthearted banter and conversation. After dinner Anna made everyone watch a program in English during which Federico seemed particularly tortured, but was genial enough in his grumbling. We settled on a date and would begin actual lessons the following Monday.

I waited until I was home to let out a whoop of joy, dancing merrily around the apartment with Cinder. Work, at last! *'Cause I've got a golden ticketttt!*

❖   ❖   ❖

Monday quickly became my favorite night of the week. The kids eagerly absorbed their new knowledge of English and the lessons proceeded with ease, but for me the highlight was the dinner conversation. Federico, whom I found intimidating at first, was, in fact, just as warm as Anna, and his good-natured ribbing about Anna's pronunciation became a part of each meal.

"It must be the British English," I said in jest whenever she flubbed a word.

"She's told us that her English is perfect," Federico was fond of saying, "but now hearing you, I realize she's just been lying to us all these years." His love for his wife was evident in his gestures, and Anna responded with her own parries whenever she came up with a word that the others didn't know.

The differences between the British English the kids were being taught in school and the American English they were learning from me made for amusing dinnertime conversation. The discussion of *eraser*, which is "rubber" in the U.K., got a huge round of laughter from Federico and Francesco when I explained that it was a slang word for condom in America. The laughter continued when I contributed my own embarrassing anecdote of how on my first trip to Tuscany, I was curious about sulfites in the wine and had inquired if the bottle had *preservativi*. Italian for condoms.

One afternoon, Anna cut our lesson short so that Francesco could watch part of the winemaking process, and she treated me to a tour. The grapes from their estate in Maremma had just been harvested.

"They are ready earlier than the Sangiovese grapes, which will be ready to harvest in a few weeks," Anna told me, waving her hand at the expanse of grapevines that surrounded us. Anna walked me through the process of separating the grapes from their stems and showed me each piece of the mammoth machinery being used. "It's all sent through these tubes, down into tanks below for the next stage."

"Where the women will stomp them," I joked. Anna smiled, but I could tell she didn't get my humor.

Anna's understanding of the earth and its products was amazing. Each meal ended with some fruit or nuts that were grown on their property. I ate their plums, figs, and jujube and was honored with the first walnuts of the season. "This is a tradition here," Anna said as she handed me a nut and a cracker. "It's good luck to have the first walnut of the season."

As she opened hers, a tiny green worm wiggled inside. My stomach churned, but she calmly plucked it out and put it aside. "The worm means it's fresh," she said, biting into the nut. In my world, the sight of a worm in nuts or produce means "chuck it," but I gamely opened my nut. Mine was thankfully worm-free, and I made my wish.

Anna also helped flesh out my Italian education by constantly explaining for me customs and traditions of Tuscany as well as giving me further insight into the people. "We aren't like the southerners," she told me one evening as we walked around the property. "We don't let people get too close. But you can know that we are always thinking of you even if we aren't in contact every minute." I had no idea as to whether Anna's assessment was true, but I thought of Laura. Maybe this explained our relationship. I had seen her only twice in my many months here, but maybe she was thinking of me? I definitely preferred the closeness of my female friendships with Cheryl, and now Bonnie, where it was OK to talk about everything, and you could email or call whenever you had something stupid or important or nothing to say.

"The people here are good people, but you'll find they gossip a lot. Talking about everyone is the local pastime of Tuscany. Don't be surprised if everyone knows everything about your life."

"That's OK," I told her. "It doesn't bother me. Who knows, maybe it will help with my job hunt? I have nothing to hide."

"Even if you did, it doesn't matter. It all gets discussed. It spreads like dandelions cropping up in a field. Each piece of news is dissected, chewed, and savored. And then it's on to the next."

She said it matter-of-factly, gazing out at the grapevines laden with maturing fruit. I noted with some irony our location and wondered if the expression about "hearing it through the grapevine" had its origins in Tuscany.

CHAPTER TWENTY-ONE

THE GRAPES OF WRATH

Despite three students for English lessons, a lot of babysitting, and some preliminary talks about the cooking school in August, by the time September hit I wasn't sleeping well. My preoccupation with money had become its own full-time job. So when I ran into the lawyer at the bar and he told me the grape harvesting would begin shortly, I said yes to being on his *squadra* with some alacrity.

And that is how I wound up in my Lucy Ricardo predicament.

So maybe back in New York I'd joked that harvesting grapes was a fallback option, but frankly, I'd never thought it would come to that. I wasn't afraid of a little hard work, but I'd also never imagined I'd be in Italy for five months and have no stable income. Will and Cheryl were the only ones who really knew how tight things were getting for me, and Will had made light of my situation with his usual sarcasm.

"I figure it's only a matter of time before you're living with Bonnie as the nanny or you've kidnapped a couple of the children and are holding them for ransom."

"The second plan won't work. I think they'd be happy to lose one or two."

And since they didn't need a full-time nanny, it was grape harvesting for me. Specifically, I was now one of *l'avvocato*'s girls. My inner feminist may have had a moment's pause at that appellation, but I reminded her that I'd voluntarily moved to a country where men still opened doors for women and never let us pay for coffee, let alone dinner. All of which I'd adjusted to quite nicely, thank you very much.

What I knew about grape harvesting was next to nothing. Removing grapes from the vines was surely involved, but I had no idea how it was actually done. I told all of my Italian friends that I was participating in the vendemmia, hoping for a few pointers, but they'd merely nodded their approval and warned me that it was tiring. Pretty much everyone had taken a turn with grape harvesting at some point in their lives, apparently. Although I could have romanticized it as a rite of passage, it was really more a means of making some quick cash for a week or two.

❖   ❖   ❖

My first day of work dawned sunny and, despite a little chill in the air, promised to be warm for late September. The cloudless, brilliantly blue sky was good news for the vineyard owners because it had been raining off and on for a week, and harvesting was impossible in the rain. Federico and Anna had explained there was only a small window when the sugar and acidity levels of the grapes would be perfect. The risk when it rained was that as the grapes grew increasingly ripe, the skin weakened and water could soak into the fruit. Our dinners in recent weeks had included a pause to watch the weather forecast for the following day. The meteorologists in Italy, on more than one station, wear official military-type uniforms, almost comical in their sobriety but seeming to inspire a level of confidence quite different from the easygoing antics and unreliable forecasts of an Al Roker or Willard Scott in the States.

The lawyer arrived at Serena's bar bright and early, and I climbed into the cab of his truck with one of his workers, Mohammad. From Tunisia, Mohammad had been helping the lawyer with odd jobs at the agriturismo. He now faced the challenge of showing this *americana* the ropes of the harvest.

"You brought clippers?" the lawyer asked me.

"No, but I brought a lot of energy." The lawyer laughed and handed me some worn red clippers, or *forbici*, that smelled as if they'd been recently oiled. I held them in my hand to get used to their weight. They would be my constant companions over the next few days. As the lawyer drove to the fields where we were to commence harvesting, I began to panic. I was supposed to be working a half-day since I had students in the afternoon, and I'd thought I could walk back from the agriturismo at the break for pranzo. But as we bounced along an old farm road, I realized we weren't starting with the vines at the agriturismo. Instead, we were harvesting a patch of land that the lawyer rented from another person. It was definitely too far to walk home. I would have to hitch a ride somehow if I was going to make it back to town.

The crew that greeted us was young. And, as the lawyer had intimated, mostly women. Most had the sleepy-eyed look of college kids who'd shown up for an early morning class after a long night. There was much yawning and brandishing of clippers as we waited for the foreman, Ernesto, to give us instructions. I'm not sure what I'd expected the harvest crew to look like, but I think I'd prepared for middle-aged immigrants or weathered, experienced Tuscans, not energetic youths. The other surprise was the presence of a couple of Americans, two cousins from Maine who were guests at the lawyer's agriturismo and wanted the experience. One in particular was raring to go. Kevin spent the whole morning outdoing everyone. He was the first to grab buckets from others to dump into the tractor, the first to volunteer whenever someone needed help. In short, he admirably represented the *americana* work ethic, even if it was a little annoying. I tried to live up to the example he set, but as a first-timer, I was a little slow in the beginning.

Mohammad planted me on the other side of the vine where he'd chosen to begin, and I trailed him down the line. He didn't explain anything, so I just followed what he was doing and filled my large red bucket. The clippers were sharp so I was quite attentive as I snipped each heavy grape cluster. I'd run into Alberto a few days before, and he'd seemed concerned I would lose a finger in the process. At the time I'd been irritated that he thought I was an idiot, but I now realized how easy it would be to snip a fingertip if you weren't careful. I held each cluster from the bottom to keep my fingers out of harm's way. The grapes were sticky and oozed juice onto my clippers and hands, making the former slippery and staining the latter an unattractive blue.

The terrain was muddy from the recent rains. Unlike the vines at the agriturismo, which were well-spaced and spanned a hill, this field was low-lying and full of bugs. The vines were ancient and looked as if they were ready for retirement. Many grapes, even to my untrained eye, seemed as if they should be discarded. But even as Mohammad told me to throw them to the ground, "*Buttale per terra*," the foreman walked by and told me to take everything. Spiders and other creepy crawlies tumbled into the truck along with the purple grape clusters.

By mid-morning everyone began stripping off layers. My bottom layer was a tank top, and as the hot sun hit my shoulders, I wished I'd thought to put on sunscreen. The work itself wasn't hard, but the constant bending position wasn't well-suited to someone tall like me. I basically walked along the vines in a permanent hunch.

We took a short break while the tractor we'd filled lumbered off, and we awaited the next. I chatted with a couple of women from Florence who came down each year to participate.

"It's not usually like this," one said when I commented that it wasn't as bad as I'd thought. "The lawyer is making his wine for the love of it, so his crew is more relaxed. At other vineyards there are people standing over your shoulder watching how fast you cut. It's much more grueling." I wondered what it would have been like if I'd been harvesting at Poliziano rather than here. Theirs was a big operation, and no doubt their crew was a well-oiled picking machine rather than this ragtag group.

As we started on our third field of the morning, I heard Kevin's cousin on my row. He was shirtless and singing along to "Ramblin' Man" by The Allman Brothers Band on his iPod. We struck up a conversation, and I felt slightly guilty for speaking in English when I saw some of the Italians staring at us.

I enjoyed listening to his Northeastern accent, which was heavy with the "Pahk the cah" inflection I remembered fondly from my undergraduate days in Massachusetts.

"We come here every year," he said, as we companionably snipped grapes and dragged our buckets along. "We've tried to do the vendemmia before, but our timing has always been off with the weather. How 'bout you? You seem to know what you're doing."

I snorted out a chuckle. "Don't make me laugh," I warned, waving my clippers at him. "I don't want to chop off a finger. Despite my attempt to look like a professional, this is my first time too."

"Are you getting paid?" he asked as he finished filling his bucket and gallantly hauled both of ours to the waiting truck.

"God, I hope so."

We finished two more rows, time flying now that I had someone to chat with. At last Kevin shouted to the group that it was time for lunch. He said it in English, but everyone seemed to understand it was time for a much anticipated break. The others abandoned their buckets and *forbici*, eagerly making their way to the waiting prepared meal. I managed to get a ride into town from one of the lawyer's housekeepers, ignoring the slight twinge in my back as I climbed into her car. A cool breeze flitted into my window as we zipped back to town. I'd successfully completed my first day of harvesting. Well, half-day anyway. Despite being tired and extremely filthy, I brimmed with a sense of pride that I'd accomplished something that would now tie me to this land forever. I'd never drink a glass of wine again without thinking of how those grapes got into that bottle.

Now I just had to survive the rest of the week. I mean, really. How bad could it be?

CHAPTER TWENTY-TWO

OUT OF THE WOODS

When it comes to my love life, my years in New York were a long walk in a dark forest, safer to keep moving forward along the visible trail than risk losing myself in the unknown depths. But something happened when I moved to Italy. For the first time in many years, I wandered off the path.

You have to flirt with Italian men. If you didn't, it would be like coming here and not eating the food or not drinking the wine. It's part of the experience. I'd flirted freely with Alberto and with Fabio (who I never saw again after he quit working at the agriturismo soon after our meeting), but it was the kind of flirting you know will never come to anything.

But the thing I like most about Italian men is that if they are interested in you, they aren't shy about saying so. And will continue to let you know until you succumb to a date with them or produce a *fidanzato* (literally "fiancé," but more often simply an exclusive boyfriend).

The cooler temperatures of September brought the return of Salvatore to the mercato. Honestly, I hadn't thought about him all summer and had established a nice fruit rapport with another *fruttivendolo* in his absence. But within two weeks of his return, we were back to bantering, and I was again the recipient of free fruit. "*Alta, bella, americana,*" he'd declare in his booming baritone when I approached. He flirted shamelessly with his blue eyes, flashing that lupine grin. Our weekly repartee put a whole new twist on the concept of meeting someone in the produce aisle.

"*Amore, voglio fare delle lezioni di inglese*," Salvatore told me one day as I stuffed gorgeous late-summer tomatoes into my bag. The older woman standing next to me raised her eyebrows, which told me to "be careful with this one" before she moved on to the fennel and spinach.

I studied his handsome face, for the first time feeling a flutter of panic at the words that would change our lighthearted relationship. I knew darn well he wasn't interested in learning English, and God help me if he was because he didn't speak a word. But his sexy grin unleashed my flirtatious side, the Jennifer Criswell who happens to be a mischievous minx, and before I knew it I'd handed him my card.

"*Chiamami quando vuoi cominciare.*" Call me when you want to start.

Tactical error! Unlike other men with whom you can safely flirt but never act on it, apparently with certain sexy Sicilians you'd better be ready for the follow-through. For the next three Thursdays at the mercato and in repeated texts, Salvatore invited me to dinner. "Don't you have a wife?" I teased one day, still hesitating to say yes. He looked at me seriously. "I am married," he said, "but I have been living here alone for sixteen years." But what about the summers? Are you separated?

I didn't ask.

Instead, I invited Salvatore to my house for dinner; I did this because I wanted to feel secure on my own turf and also because I kept picturing us in a restaurant with nothing to say. I could barely understand his deep Sicilian accent, and he had a hard time with my halting Italian. I wrote him a note, suggesting we cook something together since a lot of our brief chats centered around food. His "*sì*" was so quick that I immediately panicked, but then he offered to do all the cooking. My panic turned to intrigue.

"*Ti piacciono gli spaghetti alle vongole?*" he asked. I grinned. Was this guy for real? In America, spaghetti with clams was an aphrodisiac, but did it have the same significance here? If Salvatore was thinking along those lines, he didn't reveal it.

In profile, he bore a startling resemblance to Kevin Costner, and his blue eyes with their well-entrenched laugh lines locked onto mine with an intensity

I couldn't resist. I kept thinking this was what having a fling with an Italian was supposed to be like.

"Sounds perfect," I told him. "I'll make dessert."

✦   ✦   ✦

That afternoon, I threw myself into a frenzy of cleaning in order to make the apartment seem cozy and inviting. I mopped, dusted, scoured, and scrubbed. Had I really just invited a man I barely knew to my house for dinner? What had gotten into me? I baked an apple cake and kept myself moving so as to ignore the knots in my belly, setting the table with my pretty crystal wine glasses and arranging yellow roses in a low glass bowl for a centerpiece. I opened the wine early, ostensibly to let it breathe, but after I showered and threw on a flowered skirt and sexy black T-shirt, I poured myself a glass. Relaxed and confident was the image I wanted to project, but I felt anything but. I gulped some wine and paced. Cinder looked at me with concern: *What the hell are you up to, woman?*

When I opened the door, Salvatore kissed me and gave me an appreciative once-over that made me feel sexy and much, much calmer.

I discovered early into our evening that Salvatore did know a few words of English, but they were limited to phrases he'd picked up in his years of flirting with the women of the world. I particularly enjoyed when he called me "my darling," as if we were starring in a 1940s film.

He moved around my tiny kitchen finding the pots and pans he wanted, peeling garlic, and giving my olive oil a taste before using it. I watched as he prepared crispy calamari, slicing and flouring the rings of squid before popping them into hot oil, and as he debearded clams, tossing them into a pot with little more than red pepper and garlic for the *spaghetti alle vongole.* We explored our shared passion for cooking, and I learned about some of the delights of Sicily including *his* olive oil, which he promised I would enjoy even more than Tuscan oil. But it was slow-going with my Italian and his heavy Sicilian accent. After months of hearing the clear Tuscan enunciation, I felt as if I'd wandered into another country. He explained that he'd moved here sixteen years before because there was a demand for good produce and that he worked all the nearby markets. He was forty-eight and lived by himself in a neighboring town.

By the time Salvatore was raving about the apple cake and we'd drunk a glass of Vin Santo, I had a pretty good idea where the evening was headed. I still had some butterflies, but now they were of anticipation. The way he devoured me with his eyes made me feel sexy and desired. Salvatore kissed me with the same passion he put into his cooking, and when he grabbed my hand and dragged me toward the bedroom, I followed without a murmur of protest, more than ready to sample some more Sicilian delights.

✦ ✦ ✦

After that first evening, Salvatore and I saw each other often. He rarely spent the night because he got up every morning at four to prepare for that day's market, but a sweet text was always waiting for me when I woke up. "*Sto pensando a te,*" I'm thinking of you, or my favorite "*Ti desidero,*" I want you.

I was in a fugue of passion. Every now and again I'd wonder about his wife in Sicily and knew I needed to address it more thoroughly with him, but in those first few weeks, I didn't care. I thought of little except the next time we'd be together. I'd never been with anyone so affectionate, so unabashedly loving. We joked, we laughed, we spent hours in each other's arms talking. I felt the lock that I'd placed around my heart click open a tiny bit.

"Dance with me," Salvatore said one evening as we cleaned up the kitchen of his small house in Sarteano. We stood hip to hip washing and drying dishes. He'd lit the fireplace for me, and we'd devoured roast chicken and oatmeal cookies in front of a roaring blaze.

"There's no music, *lupo mio,*" I told him as he gathered me in his arms.

"We don't need it," he said softly as we swayed in the light of the fire.

The man wasn't wrong.

CHAPTER TWENTY-THREE

FALL FROM GRACE

The whole town knew about my affair with Salvatore—heck, they probably knew before we did.

Ordering veal at the butcher for the osso buco I was preparing for dinner felt like the "walk of shame."

Silvano gave me a knowing look. "For two people?" he asked, grinning widely, revealing the gap between his teeth. "How thick do you like them?"

I ignored his chortle and decided to take the good-natured ribbing. "I like them thick," I said without missing a beat. "Tastier that way."

Silvano snorted and laughed. He sliced the veal, content that *l'americana* was a good sport. Although I didn't realize it at the time, comments like that surely just encouraged talk about me around town.

And as it turned out, Salvatore was but the first in a long succession of Italian men who told me they wanted "English lessons." They ranged in age from twenty-five to seventy. I didn't say yes to any of the others, but I was constantly amazed at the brazenness of the ones who were married.

"*Gli uomini italiani ci provano,*" Antonella told me. And try they did. For me it was a new experience to have men let you know without preamble that they wanted to take you to bed, or as one retired firefighter told me, "*Voglio trombarti,*" an extremely vulgar way to tell someone you want to sleep with them. I actually kissed that one after I'd had a little too much wine one evening at the bar, but when he said "*Madonnina*" in the same tone as Marinella, he effectively doused any ardor I was feeling. He also convinced me to revise my feelings about *l'accento toscano*, adding the caveat that it loses some of its appeal when uttered by a man *in pensione*, no matter how handsome he is.

I'd gotten used to the sexually charged banter of my new group of friends. It ranged from a constant refrain about getting some action from their respective spouses to a more general love of sex and bawdy parlance. Every other sentence seemed to be filled with double entendre and innuendo. Even with my ongoing language limitations, I usually got the gist. For me the hardest part about attempting any sort of jokes or wordplay was that after learning some of the slang words for sex (*tromba, scopare*), I was then afraid to use them in their original meaning (trumpet, sweep), or would simply confuse the words with another. When one of my students told me he had to leave early, I'd wanted to ask why he needed to rush off, using the verb *scappare*, but out popped *scopare* instead. I corrected myself immediately, but we both had a good laugh.

One evening as Anna was driving me home after our lesson, I'd relayed my outing at the butcher and told her she'd been right about it being my turn to be the grist for the rumor mill. "In my defense," I told her, "while I knew Salvatore was married, I thought he was separated."

Or maybe I'd just wanted to believe that he was.

When I told her it had a been very long time since I'd had sex with anyone, she joked that I shouldn't tell anyone that, or I'd have a long queue of men outside my house.

"Italian men don't like the idea of a woman alone. They are convinced that she needs a man in her bed. Here, we can't go more than a month without having sex or the whole social structure will crumble."

She was only joking of course, but I had it on good authority that Montepulciano had its own official prostitute whose job over the years was to initiate the young men of the town in the ways of *l'amore*.

Wasn't there an Italian film with this scene?

Lola, despite everyone in town knowing she was a prostitute, was able to run a successful business without interference from the authorities. This was most likely because prostitution was in fact legal in Italy, as long as you weren't running a brothel, *un bordello*, which had been banned since the late 1950s. In other words, fine if you want to operate out of your home, but don't create a corporation for goodness' sake. If you look closely while strolling the streets of Montepulciano, you'll see the Vicolo dell'Amore, which was the street on which these ladies once lived.

When I asked Antonella if she thought her husband had gone to Lola when he was young, she said he'd had the opportunity but had passed.

"His dad took him and dropped him off and told him if he didn't go in, he could walk home." She shrugged. "He walked home."

"Is Lola still working?" I wondered.

"She must be close to ninety now," Antonella laughed. "But her daughter took over the business."

Of course. In a place where tradition rules and where if you make your livelihood as a butcher or a baker, you no doubt come from many generations of butchers and bakers, why shouldn't it also apply to the world's oldest profession?

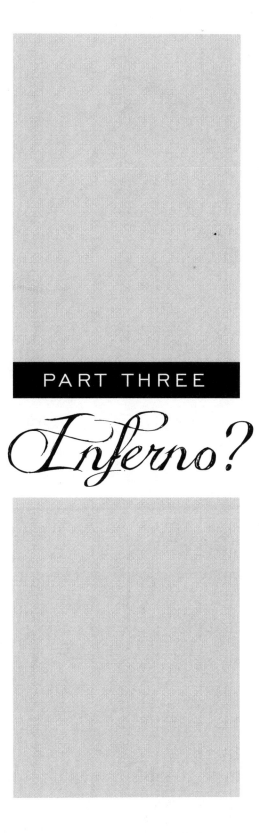

PART THREE

Inferno?

CHAPTER TWENTY-FOUR

LA NEBBIA

As the temperatures dipped, even the hot affair with Salvatore wasn't enough to distract me from my fears of surviving the looming winter. The town was shutting down, as if a switch had been thrown ending summer overnight. One week I was among a huge crowd lining the main street to watch the annual Bravio delle Botti, cheering for our respective teams as they competed in a centuries-old race pushing two-hundred-pound barrels up the long, winding hill to Piazza Grande in the late afternoon heat, and the next week it was chilly and I was buying slippers at the mercato to prepare for a winter of cold tile floors. Streets that had been full of tourists just weeks earlier were now deserted. Stores put up signs announcing they were closed for inventory or on vacation. It didn't bode well for work prospects, but it was helpful when I had the occasional babysitting job, which incidentally also had become fewer now that the kids were in school. With the streets now passable, at least I didn't have to obsess as much about Kyle trying to do a Superman leap toward speeding cars on the way to the park, and when Christopher had one of his inevitable tantrums and began wailing, I knew we weren't disturbing as many people.

White wood smoke spiraled from almost every house, little plumes perfuming the air with the scents of winter. The smell evoked comforting memories of my youth in Vermont, where a fire burned in our woodstove for most of the year. The only drawback to this odor was the laundry. With no clothes dryer, I hung my laundry outside even in winter, and if I forgot to bring it in, my clothes would smell like wood smoke at least until their next washing.

My sheets in particular always smelled faintly of smoke, making me feel as if I were on a permanent camping trip.

Even as the tourists began to dissipate, another visitor rolled into town. *La Nebbia*. The fog. A few fog-filled days had greeted me when I first arrived, but the promise of spring quickly diluted them. This was an altogether different experience . . . and I wasn't prepared. Marinella had tried to warn me. She'd been lamenting the foggy winters since August, pacing around the parking area issuing dire cryptic warnings in horror-film tones. But I didn't fully understand her concern until I was living it.

Usually, even with the rain, there was a little morning light streaming through my window as dawn broke, but the first day the fog rolled in? Nothing. As Cinder and I made our early morning foray outside, a thick mist of fog engulfed us, swallowing us whole like Jonah and the whale. The cold seeped through my light rain coat. I wished for the thousandth time that I'd brought my ugly but oh-so-toasty L.L. Bean field coat with me from New York, which had kept me warm on many a chilly morning of dog-walking and would have laughed in the face of this damp cold. I'd given it to a friend thinking that I'd surely have a job by winter and be able to afford a winter jacket.

As I carefully maneuvered the slippery bricks of our street, I felt disoriented. Utter silence surrounded me. The houses had been swallowed up, too, and our parking area was a foggy memory, literally. I couldn't see more than a few feet in front of Cinder's head. She sniffed and scented the lifelike entity as we made our way slowly up the street. Shades of Victorian London washed over me as the antique lampposts lining the street strained to emit the faintest yellow glow.

Maybe it was fitting. While I'd never considered myself a Victorian heroine prone to fluttering nerves and spells of the vapors, I was of late experiencing an agitation of spirit that would have made Jane Austen's Mrs. Bennet proud. I was staring down the very real possibility that I might be forced to abandon my dream and head back to the States. I'd done my best surviving with little to nothing, but without work, I couldn't hold out much longer.

The cooking school, for which the chef and I had prepared menus and price lists, never materialized. Apparently the lawyer had lost interest in the project. When I ran into him in the bar, he never so much as hinted at the amount of time we'd put into it or said why he'd changed his mind.

The baking business idea that I'd explored was thwarted by exorbitant self-employment tax and start-up licensing fees.

After my grape harvesting experience, I thought I'd find a little work with olive picking come harvest time, but as I learned from Marinella's husband, it takes seven kilos of olives to make one liter of oil. In other words, it's a lot of work for not much payout. Unless running a big operation, most people rely on friends and family to get the olives in for free. I would have been just as happy to be paid in olive oil, but you can only tell people so many times that you are available to help before you start to sound and feel desperate.

I did get to sample everyone's oil, though, from the Poliziano version to Antonella's. They were all fabulous, but if I had to pick one, Antonella's was my favorite: it was brilliantly green like fresh basil, with a sharp spiciness and long finish. Good thing I liked olive oil so much since it was rapidly becoming a mainstay of my diet. At dinner one night at Poliziano they'd served a homemade mayonnaise made with their oil, and I'd asked the cook, Tania, for the recipe. It's only eggs, salt, lemon, and olive oil, but the result was a delicacy that made even a plain dinner of boiled meat (*lesso*) extraordinary. I found it better on boiled meat nights at Poliziano to just dip whatever was on my plate in mayonnaise and not ask what it was. I'd already eaten tongue and spleen, both delicious until Anna told me what I was eating. Now I just kept my head down and tried not to think of what other body parts I was consuming.

If they ever wanted to fill my position the ad would need to read: **English tutor wanted. Native speaker preferred. Strong stomach suggested.**

At least my Monday night lessons and dinner with Anna and the family guaranteed me one substantial meal a week.

✦　✦　✦

When money starts to run out and you are surviving each week on mere morsels of work, you are ill-prepared to deal with an overdue visit to the gynecologist or an emergency trip to the veterinarian. So, of course, I had to deal with both.

Although Italian citizens can be seen by a public doctor for free in Italy, some opt to pay for private doctors both because appointments are scheduled more quickly and because a patient may get a little more personalized attention. I didn't have a choice since I still didn't have official paperwork and doubted I could waltz into the hospital and demand to be seen for free. Instead, I did what I'd done in New York, where I'd lived without health insurance for almost nine years: I waited. In New York, I'd never gone to the doctor until and unless every conceivable home remedy had been exhausted.

Unfortunately in my current situation, waiting wasn't going to solve anything; my period was late by almost a month. I'd only told Antonella and Serena, but inwardly I'd been freaking out. Salvatore and I had used protection, but it looked as if I was about to become part of that tiny but special percentage who get pregnant anyway. I'd taken two home pregnancy tests, which Serena had bought for me so I wouldn't have to endure the gossip of a *piccolo paese*, but despite the fact that they both said *non incinta*, I wasn't convinced. I shuddered to think of the fruit jokes that would be bandied about if indeed there were a little Salvatore on the way, giving new meaning to the expression "fruit of my loins." I hadn't said anything to Salvatore yet because I was pretty sure with a wife and three kids in Sicily, he wouldn't be thrilled with the news. I wasn't sure how I felt since I was so hormonal at that point I couldn't think straight. Even though I had never wanted to be a single mom, "this could be your last chance" kept popping into my head.

I resolved not to think about it, but one thing was certain: If I were pregnant and decided to have the baby, I'd have to move. I wouldn't be able to endure the whole town talking about *l'americana* who got knocked up by the fruit vendor. I kept picturing seeing Salvatore at the market each week. I'd be holding Cinder's leash with one hand and with the other pushing a stroller containing an adorable *bambina* who bore a startling resemblance to Kevin Costner in profile. At that point in the vision, I'd usually break into tears, then take a nap.

I got a referral from Marinella to a gynecologist and went to see Dr. Gentile at the medical clinic housed in a building near Serena's bar. I thought the doctor's name was a good sign for a gynecologist since it means "kind."

I discovered after waiting only two minutes for my visit that when you pay for a private doctor, you get seen right away. I also learned that there was no paperwork to fill out and that you pay the doctor directly.

"This is my cell phone number, if you need to reach me," Dr. Gentile said at the end of our appointment. She was in her fifties, blonde, and fairly chatty for a doctor. I liked her right away. She said *benissimo* a lot whenever I asked her a question, which means great. She showed me the ultrasound picture she'd taken during the exam, and I asked her if everything looked normal. "*Benissimo.*" I carried around her number for days and then programmed it into my phone. I felt better knowing I had my own private physician at the ready.

So I wasn't pregnant. Apparently my body was just in shock after a long hibernation. *Benissimo.*

Cinder was probably just as traumatized by her visit to see Giacomo, Marinella's veterinarian son. I'd tried for a week to ignore her head-shaking and scratching, first pleading with her not have an ear infection because I couldn't afford to take her to the vet and then when that didn't work, praying to all the Marys around my apartment. Cinder was prone to allergies so I gave her some Benadryl and hoped for the best. Unfortunately, whatever was going on wasn't getting better.

Marinella offered to drive us out to the veterinary clinic, a few miles away in the countryside. A cluster of cypresses, visible from the parking lot, seemed close enough to touch and were like sentries huddled around having a coffee break. The air was crisp and cold, but the day was thankfully sunny, fog-free. I'm not sure if this soothed Cinder, but it made me feel a little better.

We shared the tiny waiting room with a beagle in for a follow-up visit after a *cinghiale* (wild boar) attack. My neighbor's hunting dog, the one I called Zitto, had also been sporting a large bandage in recent weeks, he, too, a victim of a cinghiale. I'd noted that the hunting season seemed to coincide with the fog rolling into town. Perhaps it was Mother Nature's way of evening the odds for the beasts being stalked? Each day, early morning silence was broken by the blasts of hunters' rifles as they sought out *lepre* (wild rabbit) and various birds. I felt especially bad for Zitto since he and Alrigo hadn't even been hunting cinghiale, which was not yet in season. Apparently they'd just come across a mom protecting her babies.

As we waited, I scanned my limited but growing Italian vocabulary to try to figure out how to explain Cinder's symptoms and, if possible, to sound as if I knew what I was talking about. Giacomo, looking much more dignified and older in his doctor's coat then he usually did when I saw him heading to his car with his gym bag, brought us into the exam room. Unfortunately for him, Marinella undermined his authority by noticing that he'd buttoned up his lab coat incorrectly—nothing like having your mom embarrass you at work. He shot her the universal "*Mom*" look, and she quickly retreated to the waiting room.

While Giacomo examined and cleaned Cinder's ears, I told him nothing had changed in her diet except for a few new treats that the sweet woman from the pet store had given us. But Giacomo confirmed she had an infection, probably brought on by a food allergy. "Just kibble from now on," I threatened after the exam, as I practically lay across her body while Giacomo trimmed her absurdly long nails, which never seemed to shorten. In New York it took four techs to accomplish this task.

"*Bravo,*" I said to Giacomo, telling him about Cinder's New York experience in my improving Italian. He seemed pleased, even if he didn't say much. The nicest thing was that he refused to take any money for the visit, so I just baked him some chocolate chip cookies as a thank you. He gave me a prescription for ear drops, and when I asked where to have it filled, Marinella told me to take it to the pharmacy—the same one where the people go. I thought she was kidding.

"The animal medications are in the same place with the people's?" I asked, three times. By now she was used to the fact that I didn't always comprehend everything so she patiently repeated, "*Sì, lo stesso posto.*"

The Italian pharmacy was quite a different experience from the "Come on in and browse" type I was used to, with loads of brands to choose from and acres of aisles. Here it was spare, sterile, and pretty much everything you needed was behind the counter, where you were forced to ask a stern, white-coated woman for even the simplest things like ibuprofen. On the plus side, for condoms, you needn't suffer the embarrassment of asking—a vending machine on the wall outside was open 24/7 for your buying pleasure . . . or for hers.

As I walked in to fill Cinder's prescription, I saw an old man in the back and couldn't help but think of the scene in *It's a Wonderful Life* when the pharmacist mistakenly fills a prescription with poison and almost kills a patient. It still seemed a little risky to be filling animal medications next to people's but as I continued to discover, it was one more thing about Italy that while being different seemed to work *benissimo.*

CHAPTER TWENTY-FIVE

DICKENSIAN CHRISTMAS

It was beginning to look a lot like Christmas, everywhere except my apartment. I did have some green fir-like stuff growing, but not a live Christmas tree like the ones I'd been coveting. This was mold. With the constant humidity from the fog, the house was full of green growth, or as they call it here, *la muffa*. The three-foot-thick walls that kept the house so cool in the summer had now turned the apartment into a moist, almost sauna-like environment. And the mold thrived in it. Greenish-black and musty-smelling, it multiplied daily like some out of control science project. The areas around the electrical outlets and the wall behind my armoire were particularly appealing to it. A damp cellar odor assaulted me whenever I opened the armoire to retrieve clothes or shoes. We had a little game, the mold and me: I'd clean it off with bleach, looking like a loon from a comedy sketch as I tried to avoid inhaling the fumes by taking big gulps of air, scrubbing while holding my breath, and then rushing away to breathe. Gulp. Scrub. Breathe. Repeat. I'm sure there was a better method, but this seemed to work well enough. That is, until the mold would respond by reappearing in a week or so, an unwelcome holiday visitor. Well played, mold. Well played.

I consoled myself by planning to make my place look a little more festive with a small Christmas tree. In Italy, live Christmas trees are sold potted, so Marinella offered to take me to the nursery down the road to find one.

Then one afternoon my personal scrooge, Luciana, dropped by with the gas bill. I handed over my "holiday money" into her eager, outstretched hand.

"*Buon Natale,*" she offered as she slunk away, leaving no crumbs for a mouse—particularly cruel since I'd set the thermostat at a chilly, I-can't-believe-I haven't-gotten-pneumonia-yet fifty degrees in an effort to keep costs down.

My holiday ornaments, which I'd shipped from New York, twinkled sadly from their box. And yes, I realize you have to doubt the wisdom of a woman who brings all of her holiday ornaments to Italy but doesn't pack a winter jacket.

Christmastime just depressed me; besides not having my family and longtime friends nearby, there were none of the usual Christmas trappings. Not just the Christmas tree, but all the rest: lights, carols, sappy classic movies, baking. In New York, I'd had a highly anticipated annual Christmas party, cooking and baking a ridiculous amount of food for fifty or so friends and clients who would squeeze into my tiny apartment.

But this year I was alone. I checked in regularly with Cheryl and Will in New York, and they filled me in on their holiday festivities, recounting the turkey they'd made together for Thanksgiving. Were they missing me? I wondered. Despite a few decorated trees in front of some of the stores here, one aisle full of decorations at the supermarket, and some white icicle lights on the main street, it just didn't feel very festive. Everyone was still working. Christmas would be a dinner and a little time off.

Outside her store, Antonella had placed a beautiful little tree decorated with dried orange slices and tiny red ribbons—the prettiest on the block. She kept it in her garden the rest of the year and then brought it into town to be decked out for the holidays. Her store was stuffed with holiday goodies beautifully wrapped in Christmas paper, and I actually did feel somewhat merry when visiting with her. I spent the better half of one morning helping her make display space for the delivery of holiday cakes. The traditional domed cakes—*panettone,* speckled with raisins and candied fruits, and *pandoro,* a rich buttery sponge cake dusted with powdered sugar—took up a full shelf of the store. I amused myself picturing them being brought to a family gathering, the children's eyes wide with anticipation as they awaited a slice for dessert. The store was also stocked with brightly foiled chocolates and other confections I think Antonella ordered because she knew Bonnie would snap them up for the kids.

If I'd held out any hope that I might be spending some time over the holidays with Salvatore, he extinguished that with news that his wife was coming into town for two weeks and then he'd be in Sicily until after New Year's. I had by now figured out that while Salvatore lived a pretty autonomous life here in Tuscany, he was still very much tied to his family. He'd send me notes saying, "*Sono solo tuo*" (I'm yours and yours only), and then the next day remind me he'd be in Sicily for the weekend. Or he'd buy roses for me at the market and make a big show of presenting them to me, and then tell me not to call him that week because he wasn't free.

I had, in fact, become the "other woman" I'd always sworn I'd never be.

One evening just before Christmas, after he'd relayed the "We can't see each other for a month" news, we were discussing my holiday plans. I'd love to recount more of what he said, but I have no idea because I just sat there thinking, *Che stronzo.* You're such a jerk.

I fervently wished I could say I was flying off to Greece to meet up with friends, but he knew about my money situation, so it wouldn't do any good to lie. My actual plans at least now included Christmas Eve dinner with Anna and her family at Poliziano. I'd hesitated when she'd invited me because I didn't have money to buy gifts for anyone, but she'd insisted, and I was actually looking forward to it—mostly so I wouldn't have to spend the entire holiday alone.

"Anna suggested that I buy books for the kids in English," I told Salvatore as we were finishing the *pappa al pomodoro* (Tuscan tomato bread soup) I'd made in an effort to save money. I now felt like all kinds of an idiot when I'd cook dinner for him but continued to do it. To be fair, he cooked for me at his house, too, but at least he had a job.

"*Molto comodo,*" Antonella would say when I'd tell her I was preparing dinner for him again. Very comfortable. "*Perché lui non ti porta a cena in ristorante?*" She asked why he never took me out to dinner.

It was true, I'd made it very comfortable for him. We rarely went out for meals. Although I did in fact love to cook for someone else, I knew Antonella was right. Why didn't I insist on an evening out? I didn't have money for these multi-course dinners. I was eating eggs or tuna practically every day when I wasn't cooking for him.

"How much do you need?" Salvatore asked.

"How much what?"

"Money for the gifts."

"I'm not taking money from you. I'll figure something out. But thank you."

"We are friends first," he continued. "If you ever need anything, I want to help you."

Later that evening while I was cleaning up the remains of our dinner, I saw that he'd left money on the sideboard next to the bottle of wine he'd brought. It was more than enough to buy the gifts for the kids and maybe do a little holiday baking. I was touched by the gesture and resolutely pushed aside the intrusion of my cynical voice that slyly whispered "payment for services rendered."

Well, at least he hadn't left it by the bed.

+   +   +

Little did I know that my Christmas depression hadn't hit rock bottom yet; that came two days later after I wasted an entire morning traveling to Pienza to see about yet another job offer that didn't work out, this time because I couldn't work both lunch and dinner shifts as there was no late bus back to Montepulciano.

By that point, Pienza had lost its charm. I was forced to pay for a cab ride back to Montepulciano to the tune of thirty euros because there wasn't another bus cruising through until two in the afternoon. I sat in the cab contemplating my future and thinking that in keeping with my Dickens-themed Christmas, if the role of Scrooge was now being played by the restaurant owner in Pienza, then Luciana would be better cast as his money-hungry partner, Jacob Marley. I just hoped it wasn't a glimpse of Christmas Yet to Come.

I was home by ten thirty, the whole morning's adventure not taking more than a couple of hours but nonetheless completely deflating my spirits.

I kicked off my shoes and glanced at the television, which I'd left on for Cinder. Footage from New York of the Rockefeller Christmas tree being lit.

I burst into tears.

CHAPTER TWENTY-SIX

VIGILIA DI NATALE

"This one is for Maria Stella," said Simona as she passed a gift to her granddaughter. Maria Stella unwrapped it slowly, taking her time to discover another treasure, this time a lavender wool ski hat, gloves, and scarf set that she could take on their post-Christmas ski vacation. Maria Stella's brother, Francesco, had taken the opposite approach, one I, too, employed when young: tearing into gifts as if life depended on it, then after a cursory examination, discarding it and waiting impatiently for the next.

Simona, the matriarch of Anna's family, was in her sixties with naturally blonde hair that didn't dare go gray and a regal attitude that I found imposing. She was of the generation that was always impeccably dressed: matching handbags and shoes, the perfect necklace and earrings to accessorize, and capped off by a reservation of manner that came from having money. Despite the fact that it was Anna and Federico's house, it was tradition for her to hand out the gifts to the family on Christmas Eve. She had been doing the honors for about two hours now, one at a time so everyone could see what the other was opening. "We always open our gifts on Christmas Eve now that the kids are bigger and don't believe in Santa Claus," Anna had told me on the phone. "Then we can just relax on Christmas Day. Christmas Eve dinner will just be family, my parents, my sister, her husband, and their children." I didn't ask why Federico's family wasn't included, but he told me later on that he didn't have much family left.

When I'd arrived earlier in the evening, the first thing I'd noticed was the Christmas tree. Anna had done all of the decorating in the house, which was festive but not overdone. It was much like Anna herself, understated elegance, immaculately put together without looking as if she'd labored hours to achieve the effect. There was a large nativity scene in the entry hall, to which Maria Stella had added a dash of juvenile kitsch in the form of a small Michael Jackson figurine. Garlands of greens, including a kissing ball of *vischio* (mistletoe), adorned the halls. Dozens of holiday cards fought for space on the fireplace mantle, adding a homey touch to the ornate marble fireplace. The fireplace was my favorite part of the house, and I loved that we did our lessons in this room because it was always lit with a warm and inviting fire that enveloped us with a comforting scent of burning wood.

But this night the showpiece of the room was the tree. It wasn't the tree itself, which was fake, Anna having confessed that she'd gotten tired of the needles of live trees and pressed this one into service some years before. Nor was it the decorations, although the tree was resplendent in gold and russet tones and draped in a wide gold garland of ribbon that flicked and shimmered in the firelight. Gold balls, amber lights, and an ornate star at the top completed the accoutrements. But what was spectacular about the tree and what immediately captured my eye was the amount of presents flowing out from beneath its limbs. Nearly half of the living room was taken up with elaborately wrapped parcels of all shapes and sizes.

From my place on the couch, I had a good view of the action and had taken on baby duty for Anna's sister's newborn, Paolo. He was napping in my arms, and as I surveyed the room, I thought, This is what I'd hoped my first Christmas in Italy would be like. It was the Christmas of my imagination. The dinner with all of its courses, from the appetizer of smoked salmon on *crostini*, pumpkin soup topped with fresh porcini, traditional Christmas Eve fish, *baccalà in umido*, Federico's wonderful Poliziano Vino Nobile, to the rolling cart overflowing with traditional cakes and chocolates, accompanied by Anna and Simona's Vin Santo, the best I'd ever tasted. When I'd glimpsed Francesco eagerly slicing a piece of the tall *pandoro* cake, which looked like a craggy snow-covered mountain, I was reminded of helping Antonella arrange the Christmas cakes at her store and how I'd pictured this exact familial scene.

Spread out among three large couches, everyone relaxed, sated after the dinner. Simona picked up another package and paused.

"Jenny," she said reading the next gift's card and looking surprised. She was seated next to me at dinner, so I knew she knew who I was. Of course, the only thing she'd said to me was, "Your Italian is improving." I'd met Simona for the first time over the summer while I'd been out with Bonnie and could tell she found me wanting. Whenever I ran into her, she was always polite, but I got the feeling she wondered why her daughter liked me. Anna rose, took the gift from her, and brought it over to me. "This is for you," she said. "I hope it will bring you luck in the new year." She kissed me on the cheek.

I was shocked and a little dismayed that they'd bought something for me. Although I'd brought gifts for the kids, the only gift I'd been able to bring for Anna and Federico was some banana bread and Christmas cookies.

I handed Paolo to Zena, Maria Stella and Francesco's nanny, and unwrapped my gift. It was a beautiful, plush, luxuriously soft cashmere scarf in the autumnal color of a pumpkin bisque—easily the nicest addition to my Italian wardrobe to date. I draped it over my shoulders and then kissed both Anna and Federico to thank them.

The gift-giving continued well into the evening. Maria Stella and Francesco opened their presents from me, reading out loud the little notes I'd written each of them in English. I was proud of how far they'd come in just a few short months. Although I hadn't been able to find books in English, they seemed happy enough with my selections in Italian.

It was a wonderful evening, and although I was a little hesitant when Anna told me that Simona and Franco had offered to drive me back to Montepulciano, I gratefully accepted. I was feeling a little more predisposed toward Simona now that I had seen her give a gift of red underwear to everyone. Lacy red panties for Anna and her sister and adorable little underpants for the kids. Apparently it brings luck for the new year if you wear them on New Year's Eve. I realized Simona had a fun side to her. Maybe it was the spirit of Christmas or maybe she was content and mellow after a long enjoyable evening with her family, but on the ride home I sensed her softening toward me a bit too. We chatted the entire time, or rather I answered her questions, but at least it felt like a small connection.

In the end, my Dickensian Christmas, while having a few Oliver Twist-like characters and moments, was full of warm and loving people who had opened their hearts and home to me. *God bless us everyone . . .* or more appropriately, *Dio ci benedica tutti quanti!*

NEW YEAR'S MIRACLE

"It's here," my mom told me, waking me up late one evening with a call to my cell phone, something she hadn't done once in eight months because of the expense. Instead, we Skyped. We spoke once or twice a week through the Internet, and I spent half of the call watching her fiddle with the camera on her computer, usually getting little more than a glimpse of her hair or the window behind her. Most of the time, the connection was bad, and there was a delay, which always reminded me of when news correspondents spoke with someone in a remote location and had to wait a few seconds to hear the response. But at least it was free. The fact that she was spending the big bucks to call me on my cell phone meant it was important.

"We just got home, and it was here. Your document." I felt a slow surge of hope struggling to surface from beneath months of gloom. The last document for my citizenship application. The one I'd been waiting for since last spring. I'd sent a plethora of emails to anyone who would listen. I'd begged shamelessly, all to no avail. Finally, I'd resigned myself to the fact that there was nothing I could do to hasten the process. I just had to wait.

And now it was here. A late Christmas miracle.

My mom and I shared a few moments of celebration before moving on to the all-important question of how she would send it to me. Our luck with the Italian postal service had not been good. I was still waiting for my Christmas gift, which she'd mailed right after Thanksgiving.

I'd received a couple of other packages from friends without incident, the usual delivery time about two weeks. But whenever my parents shipped something, it seemed to traverse an Antarctic route before arriving in Italy. I'd had a glimmer of hope that I'd receive the Christmas package on time because my mail lady had brought me an official looking letter around the middle of December. She'd taken time out from her deliveries to read it through for me—a declarations form, wanting to know what was in the package and its value. I filled it out with the same information my dad had put on it, then ran over to the tourist office to fax it back. How exasperating that they had *mailed* the letter to me! According to the letter, the package had actually reached Milan about a week after my parents sent it. Next it had to be processed though Customs, a letter mailed to me, and then, after I faxed the information requested, delivery would take place. And yet my dad had put my telephone number on the packing slip.

Why couldn't they just have called me?

A few days after I faxed the form and sent the same information by email, I received a call from someone in Milan who asked me the same questions that I'd completed on the form. I again explained that the package was a Christmas gift and that I wasn't sure of the exact contents, but it was likely to be books in English, and if I were really lucky maybe an old winter jacket. I didn't mention the Advil, deodorant, and various baking supplies I'd requested since I wasn't sure which items you were actually allowed to send into the country. The man seemed satisfied that I was just an ordinary American and not some heiress expecting her winter delivery of jewels and told me he'd take care of it. But unless he was walking it here or passing it by hand to someone like the Olympic torch, I couldn't imagine why two weeks later there still was no sign of it. I made the mistake of going online and reading other people's Poste Italiane stories of shipments gone awry. I closed down the computer and resolved to wait. I think it's a necessary part of becoming Italian, this resignation to the interminable bureaucracy. Janet is fond of saying, "If you want to survive in Italy, you need two things: patience and a sense of humor."

"FedEx the document," I finally told my mom. It was horribly expensive to send a package "overnight," but at least the odds of receiving it would be improved.

"OK," she replied. "And I'll say a prayer."

I glanced at one of the Marys in my apartment. "Me too."

+ + +

I fairly skipped all the way to Piazza Grande to see Vania at the *comune*. I knew the offices were about to close for New Year's, and I wanted to try to get the application in right away. Anna had warned me that everything shut down from Christmas until after January sixth, *L'Epifania* (the Epiphany), for which *La Befana*, a kindly, rather ugly witch delivered small gifts to good children (bad children get coal), marking the end of the holiday season. Marinella had said Lorenzo had to work and the *comune* would have at least a skeleton crew.

Clutching the life-changing document in my hands I entered the doors of the cavernous offices. I didn't have the pit in my stomach that usually accompanied a trip to the *comune*. I seemed to live under a constant fear that they were going to revoke my residency.

It was early, but Vania was there. She had her coat half on and purse on her shoulder so I assumed she'd just arrived. Then I took a good look at her and realized she wasn't well. She was flushed, disheveled, and hacking with a cough I recognized well from babysitting Bonnie's kids. When she saw me, it probably took every ounce of her being not to groan. She'd obviously come into work, but someone must have told her she looked like death and to go home.

"It finally arrived?" she asked, attempting a weak smile.

"Yes," I told her, beaming happily. "But don't worry. We can do this after the first of the year. I just wanted to let you know."

"No," she said. "You've been waiting for this document for a long time. Let's do it now."

Evvai!

I spent the next hour watching as she prepared the paperwork for my citizenship application, her coughs punctuating each task she completed. She told me I needed a *marca da bollo*, the Italian revenue stamp without which it seems you can't do anything official in Italy. I ran next door to the *tabaccheria* and plunked down fifteen euros for the pleasure of obtaining this stamp for my application. Then Vania gave me an official receipt that acknowledged they were taking my original documents, and we were finished.

"You should receive a letter in the mail in the next month or two acknowledging the citizenship, and you will be done." I gave her a big hug and thanked her twenty times.

One or two months. That was much faster than I'd thought. Never one to learn from past disappointments, I began picturing the champagne we'd sip in the street to celebrate.

I headed back down the hill feeling as if a huge weight had been lifted from me. The fog that surrounded me now seemed less oppressive, almost friendly and supportive.

Antonella and the other girls were getting their shops in order as I arrived on the *corso*. I hadn't seen any of them since before Christmas. After the night at Anna's, I'd been hibernating. I'd left them all some banana bread and cookies on Christmas Eve and then wished them a Merry Christmas. Despite having made some friends here in town, I didn't receive holiday invitations to their homes. Unlike my own practice of regularly opening my door to Italian friends of friends who were alone for the holidays in New York, not one of my Montepulciano friends had included me in their plans. Not Laura and Marisa. Not Serena. Not Marinella. And perhaps the most disappointing, not Antonella. I had hoped at least Antonella might extend a last minute invite for Christmas Day, but *niente*.

Other English-speaking expats had told me that it was impossible to make close friends with the Italians. "You won't get past the front door," Janet warned. "I've been here twenty years and haven't been invited in for so much as a coffee." Of course, she'd also told me that she used to lock herself in the bathroom and cry each night for the first five years she lived here because she felt so isolated but didn't want Ken to know. I always thought of this whenever I felt lonely. But Janet was right about getting past the front door: it wasn't easy. Despite being close with Marinella, regularly going for walks with the dogs and talking about our lives, I'd only ever been invited in to her house twice and never for a meal. Both times had been when I'd needed help with official looking mail in Italian, and we'd enlisted her son Lorenzo for translation help. She often offered to teach me one of her recipes, but there was no follow-through.

But with Antonella, I knew I'd made a good friend. We'd gone to dinner a number of times, and she and Caterina regularly included me in their mid-morning coffee. I spent at least an hour each day chatting with Antonella in her shop, and we had shared things that only close friends do. I knew about her troubles with her mother-in-law, and she knew all the details of my affair with Salvatore.

"Christmas is different," Anna explained when I confessed I'd been surprised that hers was the only invitation I'd received. "It's a day to spend with family, so don't feel badly that you weren't invited anywhere. It wouldn't have even occurred to your friends to invite you." That made me feel a little better. A very little.

That morning, I reached Antonella's store first, the familiar baskets hanging beside the door and display of twig brooms telling me she was open for business.

"*Mi,*" Antonella said when she saw me. This is an intimate greeting that at first I thought was an abbreviated way of saying "my friend" or some such, but it actually seems to have its origins in the verb *mirarsi*, or *guardarsi*, which mean to look at oneself. Kind of like, "Well look who's here!"

"Where have you been hiding?" she asked, as she unloaded the bread that had just been delivered. The hard loaves clattered loudly as they fell from the bin into their wooden drawer.

"Just doing some writing," I lied, not wanting her to feel badly that I'd spent my Christmas alone with Cinder, eating reheated lasagne, which I'd stowed in the freezer for just such an emergency.

"Wait here," she said, ducking out of the shop for a minute. She returned with Gabriella and Giulia, who fills in for Caterina at the cheese shop on

Caterina's day off. "We have something for you." Antonella went into the back of the shop and emerged with a large red gift bag. "You're always bringing us cakes and cookies, so we wanted to do something for you. There is a little something from each of your favorite shops. Even the butcher."

I took the bag, speechless. I certainly hadn't expected any gifts from anyone, and all I'd given them were some baked goods. I was touched and had to choke back tears as I knew this would only make them uncomfortable. I hugged everyone, then we huddled around the stoop outside so Gabriella and Giulia could smoke while I opened my presents. I laughed when I saw that it was all of my favorite foodstuffs. My friends knew well my lack of funds, so this made the gift that much more precious. There were biscotti and *ragù di cinghiale* from Antonella, a bottle of wine (Poliziano, of course) and some honey from Caterina and Giulia, a huge salami from Silvano that caused everyone to crack wise, and from Gabriella, a beautiful recipe journal. Everything was wrapped perfectly as only the Italians can do, making even the ordinary seem special. Here, wrapping is an art form. You don't walk out of the pharmacy with aspirin without it being specially wrapped for you.

I thought of my bulging tissue paper-wrapped banana breads, which had looked as if a four-year-old had prepared them, and wondered if I'd ever gain this talent of precision wrapping. My method involves a lot of ribbon to disguise my incompetence.

I finally remembered my good news about the citizenship application, and we exchanged hugs once more after I showed them the official receipt. I allowed myself the moment to feel content and relaxed. Despite the dire warnings about Italian friendships, I felt like I'd made some good friends in Italy. They may not be overly vocal about it, but to me, it seemed appropriate that they demonstrated it with food; it's the Italian way.

CHAPTER TWENTY-EIGHT

THE WINTER OF MY DISCONTENT

The old people were in hiding. Like celebrities going into seclusion for months at a time to battle their addictions, the elderly of Montepulciano seemed to have adopted this approach for battling the winter elements. While I regularly slipped and fell on the ancient icy bricks of my street and on the steps behind the parking area, my neighbors had a better solution: they stayed inside. Why risk a fall when you could huddle beside your woodstove or fireplace and be toasty warm?

There were signs of life—huffing and puffing chimneys, the occasional crocheted curtain drawn back by curious eyes—but otherwise my block was a ghost town. The only advantage to this was that there were fewer people to witness my wipeouts, one of which was an extended slow-motion affair in which I succeeded in pulling my poor pooch down with me.

But icy slips and falls were nothing next to my most spectacular expat moment of the winter, forever to be known as The Day the Laundry Froze.

The day had started normally enough. After a quick check to make sure Marinella had put out her laundry, I'd washed a load, too, and prepared to hang it outside. I had little hope of everything drying with the limited winter sun, but if the wind was frisky they'd at least be dry enough to finish on the radiators.

I had clipped the sheets and duvet on the line, then I went about my day.

I was expecting Salvatore in the evening so we could talk. It was time to end this romance. We were still spending a lot of time together, and we had both gotten attached. I got it in my head to do the Band-Aid rip that day. The affair was just not something that could possibly go anywhere.

And while Salvatore had been a nice distraction from my poverty, I needed to face a grim reality: I was hanging on by my fingertips. My bank account was empty. Meals were spartan: an egg, pasta with a few drops of precious oil, or the now dreaded but always economical tuna. Meat was all but nonexistent; Cinder and I carefully divided our remaining stash of salami like Silas Marner hoarding his gold.

To compound my financial problems, Anna's family was on their ski vacation for two weeks, so no English lessons, and Bonnie's family was in Paris, so no babysitting. I was facing almost a month of no income. I tried to find some peace staring at my beautiful Tuscan hills, but it was not forthcoming.

Whether you are in Tuscany or in any other place, if you don't have money to live, your outlook is going to be bleak.

I thought of the many shopkeepers I'd approached over the prior months. I knew they hired people under the table, but despite repeated requests no one wanted to hire me *in nero*. I still had no idea why except that maybe they felt it was too big a risk because I was American? I thought of the blue-haired Veda and how over the summer I hadn't been desperate enough to want change old lady diapers. Now it was too late. Both of the women had since passed away. I hadn't seen Veda in months, and I pictured her in the south of Italy sitting on a beach, blue hair tucked under a straw hat while she sipped *limoncello* and enjoyed a long overdue vacation.

I began emailing friends in the States, tentatively enquiring if there might be a couch with my name on it in case I had to return. It was the first time I'd really admitted out loud, or at least in writing, that I might not be able to do this. It wasn't like in New York where even when it had been really tight, I knew I could always walk into a fast food restaurant, bookstore, or a temp agency and find some work. Here there just didn't seem to be anything.

My friend and writing mentor, Carol, was the person who set me straight after reading one of my pathetic emails. Her response was a little bit "snap out of it" coupled with some tough love:

Jen, Bella,

Hey! Wake Up! You are not a lost little orphan Annie! You are a woman who has had the guts to put her dream on the map! Yes, you are in a valley—or it feels like a valley—it's just an incline down but that same incline goes up again! There is always a gap between The Dream and The Reality.

You're at the Eleventh Hour which means all seems to be lost when the heavens open up and the next step is right there. Kermit (my father who gave me the ten things I needed to know about The World) always said, "Money doesn't disappear in a bad time, it just goes underground"—you have tons of resources, one of the reasons you are so admired—

Tons of resources? If they were here, they were buried deeper than an Etruscan tomb. But the email energized me and was enough to get me thinking and to start making a plan.

The first thing I needed to do was find a cheaper apartment. That meant giving notice to Luciana and putting out the word that I was looking. With my deposit back from Luciana, at least I'd have a little money in the bank. This would only be helpful, of course, if I managed to survive the rest of the winter.

I dreaded asking my parents for help, but in the end I did. I didn't ask for much, only a small loan to cover the rent for two months. I listened as they lectured me, thirty-nine years old, on responsibility.

"You're on a long vacation, and now you expect us to pay for it," my dad said heatedly.

As you might imagine, I didn't take that well, pleading my case loudly with the top of their heads through the computer. In the end we settled on a tiny amount of help, the sum of which I would repay with interest and for which they asked me to sign a promissory note.

My Italian friends didn't get it. Well, there was a lot about Americans they didn't get, but parents who would "loan" and not "give" money to their daughter just wasn't the norm here. I finally gave up on trying to explain the differences in American families in general and mine in particular because the gap was too wide. Here it was common for children to live with (and off) their parents well into their thirties. Italian banks were rich, Anna had told me, because there was a lot of money being saved first by frugal parents and then by the grown children who didn't have to pay for much other than an occasional vacation.

So, with the small loan from my parents, the prospect of getting back my deposit from Luciana, and generous discounts from both Salvatore and Antonella on fruit and groceries, it seemed I might be able to hang on a bit longer.

When Salvatore called to say he was on his way and bringing pizza, I finally remembered the laundry.

It was dark.

It was really cold.

It was too late.

I opened the window and stretched out to grab the duvet and heard a cracking sound, like a tree branch splintering. I tugged, but the duvet wouldn't budge, frozen solid over the line. I immediately began to panic, not because the laundry would be ruined but because I was sure all of my neighbors were at their windows witnessing my idiocy. I cast a hurried glance at Marinella's kitchen window, but thankfully the shutters were closed.

I continued to tug furiously at the duvet, the cracking noises seeming to echo accusingly throughout the valley. *Idiotaaaaa! Idiotaaaaa!*

Finally, I realized that if I lifted it straight up, I could haul it in the window. The frozen duvet was rigidly stiff and didn't want to bend to the dimensions of the window, but my mortification gave me strength and an adrenaline rush, and I yanked it inside. I could no longer stifle a laugh when I saw it standing on end. Quickly, I repeated the process. Crack. Pull. Yank. I dragged all the pieces through the window and positioned them near the radiators to encourage thawing. My apartment was now occupied by a linen regiment preparing for war, crouched and stiff, ready to advance. Cinder, who had hightailed it to her bed when she heard the first monstrous *CRACK* now gathered the courage to cautiously approach the hulking sheet fleet. She sniffed. They were menacing but obviously posed no threat. She yawned and retreated to the bedroom.

Of course, it was at this point that the doorbell rang. There were no closets in the apartment, so any hope of hiding my handiwork faded fast.

"*Buona sera,*" Salvatore said, kissing me, and assessing the situation with one glance. "*Che hai combinato?*" His look was vaguely incredulous as he waved a wine bottle in the direction of the laundry, asking me what I'd done. Then he began to laugh, first a chuckle then so hard I feared he would drop our dinner. I quickly rescued the wine and two pizzas, which I knew would be *quattro stagione*, adorned with toppings that represent each of the four seasons, and set them down before joining in the laughter.

"You don't put laundry out when it's below one degree, *amore mio*," he said, his booming baritone laugh continuing. He enveloped me in his arms. "*Alta, bella . . . americana.*"

"Don't forget *pazza*," I added. Crazy. I would forever remember if the temperature dipped below freezing not to hang the laundry outside.

Thanks to the laundry debacle, the mood was light and easy as we munched our pizzas. By now, I was used to the local way of cutting pizza with a fork and knife and rotating the plate around, one pizza for each diner. Salvatore never ate the crust, carefully carving it off and pushing it aside in a manner I always found endearing.

We agreed that remaining friends was the most important thing, and he repeatedly said he wanted to give me free produce for the rest of my life. While this was sweet, I didn't feel right about that, but I did say I would be OK with a generous discount. His face went dark, and he stared at me in silence. Perhaps my refusal had insulted him? The line from the film *The Princess Bride*, "never go against a Sicilian . . ." flitted through my brain. But I was Sicilian, too, even if it was three generations removed, so I held my ground and looked at him steadily.

"*Tre euro,*" he declared at last. "*Per tutta la vita.*"

"*D'accordo,*" I agreed. I was losing a lover, but at least I wouldn't starve.

Or as Will offered when I told him of my lifetime of produce for the low, low price of three euros: "Now you just need to find a butcher."

CHAPTER TWENTY-NINE

IL NASTRO ROSSO

After my wake-up email from Carol, if I had been waiting for my climatic turning point, like that of a novel after which you know everything will be resolved satisfactorily, those hopes were dashed by Vania one blistery day in late February.

"There's a problem," Vania said before I'd barely uttered my "*buongiorno*."

She looked much better than when I'd last seen her. She was still a bit pale, but I attributed that to her working all day in a windowless room of a dark Renaissance *palazzo* rather than any lingering pestilence. I'd just popped in to let her know I still hadn't received any notification of my citizenship, but she'd obviously been expecting me. Her tone was matter of fact, placid, an employee of the state resigned to being a cog in the wheel of a slow-moving bureaucracy and knowing full well its limitations.

She ignored the panic on my face and continued, "There is an old Italian law still in effect that says when your grandmother married, she gave up the right to pass on the citizenship. In effect, because she was a woman. The constitutionality of the law has been challenged many times over the years but has never been overturned. Your documents are now with the Ministro dell'Interno and awaiting review. It could be another seven or eight months before we hear anything. The positive news is that other people in your situation have been granted their citizenship, so precedent is on your side. Now we wait."

Hysteria bubbled up inside me as I walked out of her office. So much for a champagne celebration in the street. Vania had mentioned this law before I'd even moved, but when I'd asked if I should start gathering documents on my grandfather's side, I was positive she'd told me to wait because the law had been overturned. It didn't matter. There was no way I could possibly survive another seven or eight months if I couldn't work. As I emerged into the biting wind of Piazza Grande, I briefly considered a leap from the *comune*'s bell tower but then remembered all of the stairs I'd have to climb first.

I wanted to scream into the valley, but I threw my pumpkin bisque-colored cashmere scarf around my neck and just continued down the hill instead. Since I had adopted the "no more tears on the *corso*" rule, any crying would have to wait until I was safely back in my apartment.

✦ ✦ ✦

A few days later I was back at the *comune*, this time with reinforcements. I'd relayed my upsetting news to Anna and Federico at our Monday English lesson-cum-dinner, and Anna had insisted on accompanying me to talk to Vania. I knew Anna and her family had influence in the town, but I worried that if she upset Vania, I'd be sent packing.

When we entered Vania's office, she was in the middle of a meeting, head to head with another employee pouring over some sort of spreadsheet. She apologized and said she was on a deadline and didn't have time talk. I was ready to slink away, but Anna didn't budge. She was polite and sweet, but she stayed rooted to the floor. I wished fervently to disappear. After a minute or two, Vania gave in, and she and Anna discussed my situation in a very rapid Italian that I could barely follow. My Italian was improving daily, and at some point over the winter I'd actually begun thinking in Italian, but I still emasculated nouns on a regular basis and had trouble with fast conversations. I picked up enough to know that Vania was repeating what she told me, and that Anna was impressing upon her that I was the English teacher of her children and that she wanted to make sure I had no problems with my residency.

Vania finished her recitation and Anna nodded as if she understood the entire picture and then said, "But she needs to work while she waits, Vania. Can she work?"

My ears perked up at that.

Yes, can she?

In Italy, explained Anna after the powwow, while a case is pending before a judge as mine was, there is a presumption that they've decided in your favor. In other words, for the next seven or eight months, I could work.

I could work!

If they eventually decided not to approve the application we'd go from there.

"Plan B," Anna joked, "an Italian husband." Little did she know I'd been checking out the old men at Auser to see if there were any worthy candidates with one foot in the grave who might want to marry an *americana*.

I wasted no time in spreading the word that I could now work. My first stop was Marco Ercolani at Pulcino, who'd been telling me for months to come see him when my documents arrived.

"I've just taken on two girls this week," he told me when I shared my news. *Completo.*

I was disappointed but continued on, sure that someone would be delighted to employ me. But the responses were a replay of the year before. *Crisi. Completo.* Either no one was ready to hire yet, fearing another slow tourist season or they'd just finished their hiring but were happy to take my number. The amount of near misses was dizzying.

I got as far as a start date with the local nursery. Marinella had taken me down there to speak with the owner, Signor Galli. Both she and Janet were now engaged in some sort of unspoken alliance to help me survive. At times it seemed almost like a competition. If Janet suggested a place to try for work or made a phone call on my behalf, Marinella would counter with one of her own. If Janet invited me to lunch and I mentioned it to Marinella, she'd be over directly with some of her ragù. When Marinella found a new apartment for me across from her house, Janet came by with beautiful curtains for all of the windows. Between the two of them, I was beginning to really feel as if I now had a family in Italia—one that cared enough to make sure I wasn't going to starve or go homeless.

I did feel slightly guilty when I'd come back from a Sunday lunch at Janet's smelling of roasted chicken or lamb and Cinder would look at me as if I'd betrayed her.

Don't worry, I'd assured her, *once I'm working at the nursery, there will be plenty of money for roast chicken for both of us.*

I loved flowers, but I didn't have *un pollice verde* (green thumb) despite my continual attempts—the basil I'd planted on the terrace the previous spring had died a painful death as I tried to resuscitate it, first with too much water, then not enough. Nevertheless, I was eager to learn and tried to convey a lot of enthusiasm for what was likely to be a menial job shoveling manure and watering plants. Give me the pitchfork; I was ready.

Signor Galli, a kindly and elderly Italian, had worked for many years in Germany and told me it would be a pleasure to help someone in my situation. He collected my *carta d'identita* (ID card), *codice fiscale* (tax number), residency papers, and passport, told me he thought I'd be happy working there, and that I could start the following Tuesday.

But on Monday he called echoing the fateful sentiment of Vania and the Apollo 13 astronauts: "We have a problem."

He told me I needed a *permesso di soggiorno* (stay permit) to work for him. Apparently he spoke with someone who wasn't satisfied with the documents I'd provided. I explained once again that I didn't have a *permesso* because I was waiting for my citizenship and the *comune* had instead given me residency. I called Vania, and she offered to make an attestation that I was here legally, but Signor Galli was unmoved.

No *permesso*, no pitchfork.

I was inconsolable when I relayed the news to all of my friends who just the day before had been wishing me *auguri* on finally finding legal employment. I clutched the attestation from Vania in one hand and haltingly explained what had happened. Once again, tears flowed freely down my face in the middle of the *corso*, aka the Boulevard of Broken Dreams. There went my rule about not crying in public. In fact, soon they would have to rename the *corso* "La Via delle Lacrime Americane," the Street of American Tears.

Everyone encouraged me to keep looking, and I did, but at this point, the last vestiges of optimism had deserted me. If Signor Galli had a problem, they were all going to have a problem. Another difficult year of babysitting and teaching English loomed ahead like an unscalable mountain, with proper employment tucked safely out of reach on the other side.

Something positive needed to happen. And soon.

CHAPTER THIRTY

SCANDAL IN A SMALL TOWN

"*Stai attenta,*" Serena warned in a low voice when I arrived at the bar for my mid-morning coffee. Her tone was ominous. She glanced around the dining area, which only had two or three people in it, then told me she needed to talk to me but to wait outside. I pulled Cinder away from the garbage can where she'd just snagged the remnants of someone's cream-filled brioche and found a sunny spot in front of the bar. I immediately felt a sense of dread but had no idea what I should be careful about.

The day was shaping up to be beautiful, a brilliant sun shining overhead. It was the middle of March, and the week before, we'd been hit with a huge storm that dropped three feet of snow over three days. "Never seen anything like this in March in all my years," was the constant refrain. Even my weather maven Marinella seemed at a loss to explain what had happened. A snowstorm is one thing, but after a relatively mild winter that had been damp, gray, miserable, and long, this was particularly egregious. The snow was beautiful but heavy, and many feared that some centuries-old roofs might give way under all the weight.

Miraculously, we hadn't lost power in town, but the area around San Biagio had lost theirs for a day. Our biggest concern had been digging out. The regular snow plow couldn't fit down my street, so we were last in line for any sort of visible path to trod on. Alrigo and other men of the block obligingly took to their shovels, carving a path along the street near the houses so we could all go forth in search of supplies. It was quite sad when a good Samaritan's plow came through later that day, undoing all of their hard work and pushing three feet of snow in front of all the doors. Alrigo was undaunted, however, and continued his shoveling.

I discovered the downside to having a terrace when I was forced to attack the mounds of snow blocking me in. I didn't have a shovel, so I'm sure I was quite the sight as I cleared a path with my broom. Tedious as all get out, but eventually Cinder was able to make her way to a spot to pee. With her aging, arthritic limbs, she managed to get stuck a couple times, and I had to heave her out. We shared a moment of sadness for the loss of her youth. In her prime, Cinder loved running and leaping wildly in the heavy snow falls of New York. Now she just looked at it wistfully, leaving Marinella's dog Ozzy to do the leaping. She was like an old woman overly conscious that a bad fall could break a hip.

But this day was sunny and warm and held the promise of a long overdue spring. Snow still clung stubbornly to rooftops, and it would be another week before it was completely gone and longer still for all of the downed trees to be cleared. But as I leaned against the side of the bar and held my face to the warmth of the sun, I felt some lightening of spirit at the prospect of warm weather.

When the bar emptied out, Serena joined me outside. Her news was enough to have me seriously contemplate crying "uncle" and leaving Montepulciano for good.

"Stefano overheard two men talking about you," she told me as she sipped a concoction of milk and pear juice, which looked disgusting. "They said you were *facile*."

Easy? Me? Clearly they were confusing me with some other American.

"They must have been joking," I said, feeling all the warmth drain out of me. "I've been here a year, and I've only gone out with one man."

"A married man," she said, as if I needed reminding. "I'm just telling you so you can be careful about whom you talk to. *Piccolo paese.*" Small town.

Despite my prodding, she didn't have any further details. I went home, numb and distressed.

It was official.

I'd now entered Dante's Ninth Circle of Hell.

I knew it was commonplace here to talk about everyone, but that someone would say something so ugly about me seemed unfair, not to mention absurd. If they only knew how opposite the truth was! I spent most evenings at home, reading, with a huge dog lying beside me. I had little hope, however, that the comments had been made sarcastically. Sarcasm didn't seem to be a strength of Italian parlance.

I'd never lived in such a small town before, so I'd never experienced this propensity for commenting and passing judgment on everyone. I'm sure part of it stemmed from my being new chum for the sharks. I knew people talked about Bonnie and Mark too. *The rich Americans. Why do they feed the kids pizza almost every day? Doesn't she cook? And why do they think they can have reserved parking? No one else in town does. Did you hear they rented a limousine for the eldest's birthday party?*

There was always something being debated. I shuddered to think what else they were saying about me.

Why isn't she married at almost forty? Did you know she admits that she hates to iron? And did you see her basil plants? Madonnina.

I'd spoken openly with a few close friends about my relationship with Salvatore and now was learning a hard lesson in keeping my mouth closed. But even if that was on my record, really, after five months it was still a juicy piece of news? Talk about a long, hard-up winter.

I spent the day in my house puzzling over who might have said such a thing, compiling a list of suspects. There were, of course, the married men who were constantly hitting on me in the bar, whom I had turned down. Maybe this was payback? Or what about Giorgio? Even after my refusal, he'd tried again. Or the firefighter that I'd kissed? Maybe he'd decided to spice up our encounter with a little exaggeration.

I tried to remember everything I'd done in recent weeks that could possibly have garnered some sort of attention—I began scrutinizing things I would have never thought twice about in New York. I had bought condoms at the machine outside the pharmacy when Salvatore had been unprepared. But I'd done that early on a rainy weekend morning, and there had been no one around. Or at least I didn't see anyone.

And what about the sexually charged joking and chatting with my friends in town? Perhaps because I was single and they were married, my jokes and banter weren't taken as innocently as I had thought.

There was also the time at the bar when the lawyer had asked me if I would wear a cleavage-baring top to do a wine tasting. We'd been laughing and joking, so perhaps someone overheard and then spread the word?

Or what about my English students? There weren't that many, but they were predominantly male college students who came to my house . . . for an hour. Great, now I might even have Lola's daughter upset with me, thinking I'm moving in on her clientele.

Or the red towels that I hung on the line? Perhaps they had been inflaming the passions of the men of the town like bulls in the ring?

It was all ridiculous, and after a day of driving myself crazy, I finally resigned myself to the fact that there was nothing I could do except be *attenta*.

I felt self-conscious for days when I would walk up the street as heads swiveled in my direction. Who was I now, Joan Crawford in *The Women*? Were the wives of the town feeling the need to protect their husbands from the vixen *americana*? "One fling in one year!" I wanted to shout. "I'm single! That's not 'easy,' that's sad!"

I confided in Antonella, and she tried to make me feel better. "It doesn't matter what you do here," she said. "The people will talk. They lack excitement in their own lives. Because I'm friendly and joke with my clients, people think I've slept around. It's not true." She shrugged. "You just have to live your life."

After a week, I thought maybe it was safe to go back to the bar, which I'd taken pains to avoid despite missing my morning routine. Once I thought the storm would have died down, I joined Serena for a coffee, and while we were talking, a regular came in. An older, white-haired employee of the Guardia di Finanza, his reputation was that of a *trombatore*, a modern-day Lothario.

"Those who have worked in uniform are always the worst," Antonella had told me. "They have an inflated sense of ego."

I'd spoken to this man many times, and he sometimes threw a crumb or two Cinder's way. He'd certainly never flirted with me.

But obviously word was out. "You're the American who teaches English?" he asked sitting down with a newspaper at a table next to us.

I felt my face flame. Serena gave me a knowing look and retreated behind the bar.

"*You*'re interested in English lessons?" I asked, my voice laced with skepticism. I let my gaze linger on his head with its wispy white hairs, long in the back to compensate for the rapidly balding front. Hoping for *facile*, he was sadly disappointed. He mumbled something and stuck his head in his paper.

Apparently it was going to take awhile for this to die down. I decided then and there to just let them talk; I had bigger things to worry about.

I said my goodbyes to Serena, and she asked me what I was going to do today.

"English lessons," I told her. "You'd be surprised at how many new requests I've been getting."

CHAPTER THIRTY-ONE

PRIMAVERA

"And if you look across the fields," I said confidently to the group of Americans trailing along behind me, "the hill town in front of you is Montepulciano. That's where I live." I paused to let the group, a family of six from Massachusetts, snap some photos of the fields of Sangiovese grapes that stretched out before us.

I was working! At Poliziano!

I'd almost fallen off my chair at dinner the week before when Anna mentioned that they needed someone who spoke English to cover the absence of Margherita, one of their employees who normally gave tours of the cantina and conducted wine tastings.

"It's only for two weeks," she'd told me, "but if it works out, there might be other opportunities in the future. Federico wants to try to take you on with a contract."

Evvai!

Of course, it hadn't been that simple. With the ongoing lack of a *permesso*, even Federico was stymied in his efforts to employ me through the work office in Montepulciano. The Centro per L'Impiego wasn't clear on how to give me a contract. They were like horses wearing blinders; they only knew one route to take. But Federico's office manager, Stefania, was undeterred; she had everyone making calls on my behalf. They hadn't reached a solution yet but seemed optimistic.

I trained with Margherita for one day before she departed, and then I was on my own. Well, on my own with Fabio, my boss. He handled all of the inside wine sales, the tastings with food, and lunch. Tall and robust, Fabio was also strapping, if an Italian could be strapping. His beautiful eyes were the same rich caramel color as the Poliziano Vin Santo. (Yes, this was my second experience working in a kitchen with a handsome Italian named Fabio.)

My job was to make Fabio's job easier and to take the brunt of the English-speaking tourists. Fabio spoke English, but he'd only learned it two years before, and it was mostly hospitality-based. I was only mildly offended when he said my Italian was as good as his English. He was easygoing with a perpetual smile and tendency to joke, and we hit it off immediately. He also had a charming and very pregnant wife and an adorable three-year-old, Pietro.

I didn't know too much about winemaking, but I was relatively expert in the art of the vendemmia so I was able to spice up my tours with that information. My head overflowed with the length of times the wine aged in the French oak barrels, fermentation procedures, and the percentages of which grapes were used in which wines.

I didn't always get things right.

"Erm, isn't that Cortona?" asked one of the teenagers in the group.

I glanced at the hill town in the distance and realized that I had indeed been pointing out Cortona and not Montepulciano. In my defense, Montepulciano is clearly visible from the other vineyard where I usually began the tour, and I'd just gotten turned around.

"Just testing you," I laughed easily and continued on, inundating the know-it-all with information on the green harvest in July, which was an extra step Poliziano took to weed out all the grape bunches that weren't going to reach maturity; this would allow more nutrition to get to the viable fruit. At this point, the grapes were smaller than the spring peas flooding the mercato, but the weather was warming, and they'd soon be doubling in size. The air was filled with the fragrance of the countryside, including the lavender just in bloom, and I felt an immense sense of serenity in this place. More than that, I felt rejuvenated.

I continued the tour in the cellar, explaining the fermentation process, then back up through the original stone cellar to expound on the aging process in the oak barrels, past the sleeping bottles of vino in their cages, through the library where the past vintages of the winery were displayed, until we reached the barrel room: two thousand French oak barrels in a humidity- and temperature-controlled environment where the Vino Nobile and the reserve *Asinone* were aged. The air was heady with the smell of wine. By far, my favorite part of the tour.

While I talked about the origin of the barrels, their importance, and what happened to them after their short, four-year life span, I entertained a fantasy of actually having permanent work at Poliziano. It was a quick ten-minute bus ride from town, and although I couldn't make it home at lunchtime to take Cinder out, Marinella had offered to help with that and had been taking her out twice a day. Thanks also to Marinella, I had moved into a new apartment that was on our same street and had bid farewell to Luciana. Not for good, unfortunately, as she let me know I should expect another gas bill, which she predicted would be high since the previous ones had been estimated. I'd be playing Bob Cratchit for a little while longer it seemed.

The new apartment was a little bigger than the old one and was bright and airy with four enormous windows, two of which had the same gorgeous view as Luciana's place. Best of all? No evidence of mold. That alone would have sold me on it. My new landlord, Massimo, lived in the apartment above mine and had gone out of his way to make things comfortable for me. He'd installed a washing machine from this century that totally changed my laundry experience for the better.

The six-burner stove had a gas tank inside, and I had to light it with a match, but the kitchen was big and sun-filled and with a few improvements would be ideal for cooking my expanding repertoire of Tuscan dishes. (Marinella had finally committed to teaching me a recipe a week, and I'd nicknamed our cooking days "Thursdays with Mari.")

The apartment's décor looked as if Massimo's old aunt had lived there, because, in fact, she had, but I didn't care. The price was right, the view was spectacular, and the jasmine from Marinella's stone wall now wafted into my kitchen. I'd taken to employing Cinder's method of cocking my head on every breeze, trying to catch the scent.

It hardly seemed possible that I'd now been here over a year. That I'd actually survived the winter and was looking forward to the summer ahead. New apartment, a little work, things at long last were improving.

"Excuse me, but you said that the Vino Nobile is in these barrels for fourteen to sixteen months, right?"

The teenager again.

"So how much wine is lost to evaporation in that time?" No doubt confident I wouldn't know the answer, he smirked—not a good look for him with his adolescent acne.

"We lose about thirty percent over that time," I replied. "In much the same way as in Scotland where they can lose up to forty percent of their whiskey while it's aging in the barrels, it's the same idea here. This room was specially designed to help control that loss." I only knew the answer to this question because someone had asked it a couple of days before, and we'd consulted Fabio. I made up the part about the room controlling the rate of evaporation, but it sounded good, and who knows? Maybe it was even true. So much of my time in Italy had been about improvising under the circumstances, such explanations came out quite naturally whenever I was placed on the spot.

"Any other great questions?" I asked, smiling sweetly at the kid who was now sullen. "If not, let's go taste some wine."

✦   ✦   ✦

"Are you sure you want to be an Italian?" Fabio asked one morning as we were in the kitchen preparing for lunch. I was slicing tomatoes into the precision thin slivers that he wanted for the bruschetta.

"The women are crazy for my bruschetta," he told me with a wink.

I laughed but concentrated on my slicing. While he made it look easy, it didn't come naturally to me, yet another example of Italian precision that I might never master. Italians seem to perform even the smallest task with a level of attention and care that borders on obsession.

Recently, my new friend Tiziana, who worked in the office at Poliziano and was driving me home each evening so I could avoid a second bus trip, told me that the Italians ironed even their underwear.

"It's not possible," I said dismayed at this news. "How do you have time to do that?"

She shrugged. "It's our way."

I was sure she was right about that since Fabio had already told me that if I didn't like ironing, I was going to have a hard time finding an Italian man to marry.

"Your age is difficult," he joked. "That plus the ironing . . . *Madonnina*."

"*Stronzo*," I'd retorted. "Don't worry about me, I have other talents." Then as his mouth was hanging open, I'd added, "I can cook! Get your mind out of the gutter!"

Not even being the subject of town gossip could make me stop being myself entirely, and part of that was sometimes cracking risqué jokes; I did think more about the company I was in before making them, however. Besides, I'd forgotten how much fun it was to work among people, to interact, and to feel useful. I was in the flow. What a difference a year makes.

As for finding an Italian man, I was in no hurry.

Even as the swallows were still returning from the south, Salvatore had departed on his annual migration to Sicily where he'd work in his orchards over the summer. He sent me texts frequently, and although it was flattering to hear a man continually say, "*Ti desidero*," I wasn't going back down that road. I was grateful to him for reawakening something in me that had been dormant for far too many years, but now I was content to wait. I'd reclaimed a confidence in myself that I knew I wouldn't give up again.

"If that's your way of trying to get rid of me," I said now, finally answering Fabio's question about wanting to be Italian, "forget it. Even if I have to wait three years for the citizenship, I'm staying."

And I meant it.

Obviously, the year hadn't been easy. I still felt scarred in many ways from the bruises and hits I took along the way. Walking by the *comune* still put a pit of dread in my stomach. Seeing a can of tuna made me nauseated. But I'd made it through the hardest year, beginning like a baby bird, not yet knowing how to survive but taking cues from those around me and following their lead until pushed out of the nest. I hadn't exactly soared, but I hadn't hit the ground with a thud either.

There were, of course, things about Italy I still hadn't adjusted to. I chafed at the fact that the Italians were loathe to reply to emails or even phone calls. My experience with the bureaucracy had been and still was fatiguing, to put it mildly. The post office was hit or miss. And the white unsalted Tuscan bread was still blah.

I hadn't as of yet come to terms with everyone knowing everything about my life and having to constantly censor myself before I said or did something in passing that could come back to bite me in the ass. The friendships I'd formed were solid albeit much different than those with friends in the States; in Italy, I learned the hard way that I could confide in my friends as long as I was prepared to have those confidences discussed around town.

But those were *piccole cose*, as Alberto would say.

The things that I loved about Italy were still here after a year. The landscape that filled me with contentment, waking to church bells and birds, the taste and scent of freshly harvested fruits and vegetables, the olive oil, the wine, the history.

And the people.

I'd developed a new sense of appreciation for the Tuscan people. They were hardworking Italians who understood the land and all of its offerings. They weren't larger than life caricatures; they were just normal people. Their contradictions intrigued me, and I still hadn't yet worked out how a people who had no problem eating raw pancetta and beef could refuse to drink perfectly good water from the tap; or that while appreciating the earth's bounty, they still insisted on peeling every last potato and piece of fruit, even their peaches, because they were worried about the dirt. They had a marked tenacity to preserve the past, oftentimes to their benefit, though sometimes to their detriment. They were at times wary of outsiders and anyone looking to change their way of life but ultimately were warm and caring.

Had I found what I'd been searching for? A smaller life? Definitely. I was living in a town that could fit in the palm of New York's hand. *Dalla Grande Mela alla Grande Uva,* as one of my friends put it. From the Big Apple to the Big Grape. At times I felt as if I'd moved back in time as well as to another country, but there was something very comforting in the rituals of small town life. The daily reading of the notice board, a mid-morning coffee to catch up on the latest family dramas, daily trips to the butcher or market to prepare for that day's lunch. I'd gained an appreciation of the seasons and looked forward to the produce that arrived with each change: the asparagus and artichokes of the spring; the plentiful melons and peaches of summer; the fennel, squash, and apples of fall; and the clementines of winter. I still had much to learn about the land and had an unslakable thirst for knowledge of the *contadini* and their farming of this region. I wanted to learn how to tell when the olives were ripe for picking, how to prepare the grapevines before harvest, how to make a pizza without measuring ingredients, how to grow things from the land and use all of its parts.

Piano, piano.

In time, I would learn these things. Slowing down was essential to hearing the natural rhythms around me.

I was beginning to feel a part of this community now. I'd never be one of them—our views on the world were too different—but they'd accepted me even with my strange city ideas, bursts of emotion, foreign desserts, and lack of precision.

It hadn't been an easy year and the work struggle was likely to be ongoing, but I was already looking forward to the months ahead.

L'avventura continua.

Surprisingly, despite the hardships, my inner optimist appeared to be alive and well and living her dream in Tuscany.

EPILOGUE

The immigration office in Siena is an unassuming brick building that you might miss if it weren't for the fifty or so people ready to storm its doors in the early morning hours on their appointment day. Immigrants from other parts of Europe and beyond crowded together in hopes of obtaining their *permessi di soggiorno*.

I wasn't alarmed as I waited for the doors to open at eight thirty. This was my second visit to this office and my third to Siena in the past few months.

Stefania had sat me down in her office at Poliziano during my second week of work to let me know she'd found a solution to my *permesso* problem. She'd spoken with a police officer in the *questura* (police headquarters) in Chiusi and explained the entire story—by now she knew my saga as well as I did—and the police officer agreed to help us.

My initial appointment date was June 29, and I'd arrived in Siena bright and early; I had to take the six o'clock bus to arrive at the Questura before 8:30 a.m. Janet was kind enough and maybe just a little masochistic to offer to come with me. Janet is wonderful but bossy in the best of times, so I was a little worried that she was going to say something rude to the wrong person, but after we'd munched a piece of fruit tart she seemed content to stand beside me and comment on the other people waiting with us.

Through the open door, I could see a bristly white-haired man with a trim goatee whose line was moving more quickly than the others. He was chewing gum and hustling. When it was my turn, I was sent to his line, and I answered his rapidly fired questions in Italian, with a little help from Janet. His fingers flew across the keyboard as he typed up all my information, chewing his gum all the while. He printed out a document and attached my photos.

"Just take this back to the Questura office, and they'll do your fingerprints. Five minutes and you'll be done. The *permesso* will be ready in forty days."

Janet and I beamed at the man and headed back to the main Questura headquarters near the *duomo*.

Unfortunately, it didn't take five minutes. What I've neglected to mention is that it was Palio week in Siena. The famous, historic horse race was in two days, and half the town was at the practice. Including the man who was to do my fingerprints. "You'll have to come back tomorrow," said the cute police officer at the front desk.

I wheedled, cajoled, offered a coffee, and tried valiantly to explain that I couldn't come back the following morning as I had students for an English class. Just as it seemed he would help, Janet sailed forward.

"She can't be here tomorrow, your office is closed Thursday, there's a bus strike on Friday, and," she paused to huff out a breath, "and it's the Palio." Janet's voice was rough, and I could see my cute officer's face close down.

"There's nothing I can do," he said brusquely and walked away.

As we reemerged into the brilliant June sunshine, I railed at my friend. "He was going to help us. Why? Why did you yell at him? Now I have to spend another three hours on the bus for a five-minute procedure."

After I got back to Montepulciano, of course, I saw the humor in a public office closing down so the man in charge could go to Palio practice, but that bus ride home was tense.

I sent a text to Anna because Federico had been joking that after all I'd gone through surely there would be a hail storm in Siena or some other impediment thrown in front of me. "Tell Federico that there wasn't hail in Siena today . . . only horses. *Che Palio!*"

Anna wrote back: "*Chi la dura, la vince.*" He who endures, wins.

It was now September. Fields of brown-stalked sunflowers bowed their heads permanently as they waited to be processed for their oil. Wheat fields, which had been harvested in July, had been recently tilled, exposing huge clods of earth and aerating the land before a new planting in November. Brilliant blue skies foretold crisp nights, reminding me that I needed to peruse the market for some new slippers. My second summer had flown by, a blur of wine tastings and tours with tourists, as well as teaching English to a group of elementary school kids at Sant'Agnese, a church near my house.

I'd also celebrated my fortieth birthday a few weeks back, this year slurping down margaritas with Bonnie and Mark alongside the carrot cake. I was now officially at the age that was no longer considered "young" unless you were talking about someone who had died.

My goateed, gum-chewing man was back behind the desk when I arrived at the immigration office in Siena, and seeing his efficient competence somehow gave me hope that I actually might succeed in this behemoth of a mission. When I reached his desk, he ripped open an envelope, and after checking my fingerprints against the digitized prints of the card, handed me my *permesso*.

"You're all set, Jennifer," he said with a smile.

I thanked him and waded through the other expectant immigrants with a grin plastered on my face. I was certain there would be many more bureaucratic hoops to leap through in the coming year as I waited for my citizenship to be finalized, but at least now I had something tangible to allow me to stay in the country and to work.

I sent a text to Anna and Federico to let them know I had the *permesso* in hand. They'd scheduled me to work the following week at Poliziano in optimistic anticipation of that elusive document.

Anna's words echoed through my head as I strolled through the cobbled streets of Siena, feeling a sense of acceptance and peace: *Chi la dura, la vince!*

Tension melted from my shoulders, and I allowed myself to savor the moment. I had definitely endured. And now this was my home. Tourists' voices echoed around me as I walked. While it still gave me pleasure to hear English, I now knew I could survive even without it and that I had become a fixed part of this country in a way that had seemed impossible when I first arrived. My roots had been planted and had even begun to sprout new growth.

I wandered into a small café off a narrow alley and ordered an espresso. The barista who prepared it was strikingly handsome with the light eyes I can never resist.

"*Americana?*" He smiled as he set down my coffee. He drew another cup for himself and leaned against the counter, ready for a chat.

"*Italiana*," I responded with an answering grin. "*In prova.*"

ABOUT THE AUTHOR

Jennifer Criswell is a lawyer-turned-writer who chucked her legal briefs to pursue her love of writing after a life-changing trip to Italy in 2001. Jennifer lives and writes in a small hill town in Tuscany with her sidekick of a Weimaraner, Cinder. Her website is http://jennifercriswell.com.

Made in the USA
San Bernardino, CA
23 June 2020